# Supervision for Better Instruction

# Supervision for Better Instruction
## Practical Techniques for Improving Staff Performance

## Marcia Kalb Knoll, Ed.D.

PRENTICE-HALL, INC., Englewood Cliffs, New Jersey

Prentice-Hall International, Inc., *London*
Prentice-Hall of Australia, Pty. Ltd., *Sydney*
Prentice-Hall Canada, Inc., *Toronto*
Prentice-Hall of India Private Ltd., *New Delhi*
Prentice-Hall of Japan, Inc., *Tokyo*
Prentice-Hall of Southeast Asia Pte. Ltd., *Singapore*
Editora Prentice-Hall do Brasil Ltda., *Rio de Janeiro*
Prentice-Hall Hispanoamericana, S.A., *Mexico*


© 1987 *by*

PRENTICE-HALL, INC.
Englewood Cliffs, N.J.

**Library of Congress Cataloging-in-Publication Data**

Knoll, Marcia Kalb
    Supervision for better instruction.

    Includes Index.
    1. School supervision.    2. Teachers—Rating of.
3. School personnel management.    I. Title.
LB2805.K556   1987      371.2′01      86-25188

ISBN 0-13-876426-3


Printed in the United States of America

# ABOUT THE AUTHOR

Marcia Kalb Knoll, Ed.D., is currently the Director of Curriculum and Instruction for District 28 schools in Queens, New York. She is also an adjunct associate professor in the Graduate School of Education at St. John's University and was previously an elementary principal in Queens.

Dr. Knoll also has designed and now directs a Saturday program for gifted youngsters at St. John's and is the author of children's skill books in the areas of reading and mathematics.

A frequent workshop leader and speaker at various educational conferences, Dr. Knoll is an active member of several professional organizations. She has served as a vice-president of the Queensborough affiliate of the International Reading Association and as president of the St. John's Chapter of Phi Delta Kappa. Dr. Knoll was recently elected president-elect of the national Association for Supervision and Curriculum Development.

Dr. Knoll is also the author of *Elementary Principal's Survival Guide* (Prentice-Hall, 1984).

# HOW THIS BOOK WILL HELP YOU IMPROVE STAFF PERFORMANCE

Supervision presents the school administrator with a task that is often time-consuming, exhausting, and frustrating. Yet it is the most serious responsibility any administrator can accept.

Supervision is the process of improving teacher performance, thereby making instruction more successful. You, as a supervisor, should play a vital role in each teacher's instructional effectiveness because nothing is more important than what happens in the classroom between the teacher and his or her students.

*Supervision for Better Instruction: Practical Techniques for Improving Staff Performance* addresses the supervisor's responsibility by presenting effective techniques and strategies for supervising teacher performance. Three factors contribute to making this book appropriate for *all* supervisors:

1. It deals with real supervision issues in a practical and easy-to-use format.
2. It is filled with charts and forms that clarify strategies and make application easy.
3. It presents samples and case studies of actual supervisory activities.

You can use *Supervision for Better Instruction* either as a total supervisory guide or as a means of targeting those aspects of supervision that are your greatest concern. The book is divided into six parts that, together, make up the instructional supervision process:

1. How to Establish a Standard for Excellence in Teaching
2. How to Diagnose Teacher Needs
3. How to Match Supervision to Teacher Needs
4. How to Communicate Successfully
5. How to Supervise Others Who Teach
6. How to Supervise Nonteaching Personnel

Let's take a closer look at each part to see how it will help you supervise better.

## Establishing a Standard for Excellence in Teaching

Part I deals first with the issue of supervision versus evaluation. The basic aspects of both are discussed and compared, with suggestions for taming the negative effects of evaluation.

Next, the section dealing with establishment of a standard for teaching is concerned with six specific criteria that determine excellence in teaching skills:

1. Classroom environment
2. Preparation for instruction
3. Interaction with students
4. Management of the learning environment
5. Professionalism
6. Parent/community interaction

Each of the six aspects is fully discussed, with a composite form provided as an easy-to-use guide.

Part I also analyzes many of the problems associated with pull-out programs, including concerns with schedules, articulation, communication, possible hostility between the teachers, and limited time. Specific strategies for dealing with pull-out problems are accompanied by forms that can easily be adapted for any school. Part I concludes with specific strategies for matching teacher type to the proper level of supervisory control.

## Diagnosing Teacher Needs

Part II offers specific guidelines for gathering the data needed in diagnosing teacher needs. Next, eight different techniques for diagnosing teacher needs are presented in complete detail, along with appropriate forms and step-by-step directions for their use.

The diagnostic techniques presented include exploration conferences, informal visits, reviewing teacher plans, evaluating the classroom as a learning environment, time-on-task reviews, viewing student products, formal exploration visits, and using reported data as an information source. Each technique is accompanied by suggestions for use and communication of the data collected.

## Matching Supervision to Teacher Needs

Part III details how to match supervision to diagnosed teacher needs. First, the "how" and "why" of tailoring the supervision process is discussed, followed by the three elements of a tailored supervision process: selecting the objective, selecting the plan, and inviting the teacher to participate in the plan.

Next, four different supervisory plans are discussed, each supplemented with a process for review, implementation of results, and an actual case study model. The four supervisory plans are intensive guided supervision, collaborative supervision, peer supervision, and self-directed supervision.

Part III also details your specific role in the supervision process and presents a procedure for the staff's rating of the supervisor, with step-by-step directions for analyzing, interpreting, and using the results.

## Communicating Successfully

Part IV covers the essential topic of communication, beginning with the importance of providing a secure climate in which effective supervision can flourish, then discussing essentials of this climate that the supervisor must provide. These are: an understanding of basic human needs, the fostering of feelings of security, and the reinforcement of those feelings through nonverbal communication.

The conference as a vital communication tool for transmitting feedback and forming the supervision plan is fully discussed, including an explanation of the six stages of conferencing, each with suggestions for sample language that may be used.

The next section of Part IV gives techniques for writing effective communications and analyzes the strengths and weaknesses of written communication. The last element of communication, recordkeeping, completes Part IV. Detailed forms and strategies are presented to help you keep accurate records of both a formal and an informal nature. Specific suggestions are made to help you use time efficiently and effectively.

## Supervising Others Who Teach

Part V deals with the many nonteachers who also work with students, such as teacher assistants, student or intern teachers, and volunteers. They, too, should be supervised. Here you will find a full description of their roles, and techniques you can use to evaluate their effectiveness.

## Supervising Nonteaching Personnel

Part VI is concerned with the nonteaching personnel, such as school aides, food service workers, school plant staff, and the secretarial staff—all of whom directly or indirectly affect the lives and well-being of your students. At times, the way nonteaching personnel perform their jobs has an impact on instruction and learning, so supervision of these staff members is very important. Part VI outlines the specifics of each role, and suggests ways to monitor individual effectiveness, and improve the performance of nonteaching personnel.

## A FINAL WORD

*Supervision for Better Instruction* discusses, explains, and supports three major points that all supervisors should keep in mind when dealing with their staffs.

1. Supervisory efforts are both effective and efficient when supervisory objectives and plans reflect the individual teacher's needs.
2. Supervisory efforts are enhanced when humane and precise lines of communication are used.
3. Effective supervision results in increased teacher motivation, inspiration, and trust in the supervisor.

Adhering to these concepts will help you reach your school's goal of improving the instruction that students receive.

Marcia Kalb Knoll

# CONTENTS

# How to Establish a Standard for Excellence in Teaching

# Knowing the Difference Between Supervision and Evaluation

Since this book is dedicated to the improvement of teacher performance, it is important to begin with a clarification. A long-standing confusion exists that supervision to improve teacher performance is accomplished by an evaluation of that performance. Supervision and evaluation are, however, distinctly different from each other in three important ways. (See Figure 1-1.)

The first difference centers on the objectives to be accomplished. Supervision and evaluation each focus on radically different objectives.

The second difference is based in the activities conducted. Since the objectives of supervision and evaluation are different, the activities that each uses to accomplish its objectives are also very different.

The third difference is found in the resulting outcomes. The following is a full discussion of the objectives, activities, and outcomes that make supervision and evaluation so very different from one another.

## WHAT IS SUPERVISION?

Supervision is a leadership role. In performing this role, the supervisor diagnoses teacher performance needs and then guides, directs, assists, suggests, supports, and consults with the teacher.

## Objectives to Be Accomplished

The objectives of supervision are to help the teacher learn what aspects of his or her teaching performance need improvement and then, specifically, how to improve them.

## Activities Conducted

The supervisory process begins with an identification of the areas needing improvement. These areas are identified through a diagnostic process.

### Figure 1-1

**SUPERVISION/EVALUATION COMPARISON**

|  | Supervision | Evaluation |
|---|---|---|
| **Objective:** | To improve teacher performance. | To rate teacher performance |
| **Activities:** | Identify needs of teacher | Judge performance of teacher |
|  | Focus on areas needing help | Offer global overview of teaching efforts |
|  | Involve teacher in improvement plan | Make teacher aware of weaknesses |
|  | Use objective terms | Use subjective values |
| **Outcomes:** | Motivation to improve | Demoralization |
|  | Inspiration to continue improving | Frustration |
|  | Trust in the supervisor grows | Suspicion of the supervisor results |

The next supervisory activity is to focus the improvement effort. This focus is both limited and specific at any given time. The number of areas that are involved in the improvement effort must be realistic and manageable.

The supervisory effort involves the teacher in the development of a constructive plan for improvement. The supervisor and the teacher work together to provide the resources, both human and material, which will be required to carry out the plan.

Objective terms are used when conducting the diagnosis and implementing the plan. The teacher's actions are described in terms that state what was actually seen, without drawing a conclusion. Several examples of objective language follow:

1. *"Several children in the back of the room were playing with baseball cards during the lesson."*
2. *"No one in the class responded to that critical-thinking question."*
3. *"Here are the questions you asked. Each of them required a 'yes' or 'no' answer."*

## Resulting Outcomes

The outcomes of the supervisory activities are usually both positive and productive. Because the supervisory activities foster teacher motivation, inspiration, and trust, they help the teacher improve his or her teaching performance.

Supervisory activities foster motivation because the supervisory suggestions for improvement discussed with the teacher are realistic and within the teacher's ability to implement. Therefore, the teacher is motivated to act.

When teachers are motivated they are usually successful. Success inspires people to continue their efforts, work harder on the tasks, and strive for higher goals.

The helping nature of the relationship that develops during the supervisory process results in a climate of mutual respect and trust. The teacher's individual experience with the supervisory process leads him or her to view supervision as helpful rather than harmful.

# WHAT IS EVALUATION?

Evaluation is a judgmental role. In performing this role, the supervisor examines and judges teacher performance in order to determine its quality or fix its value.

## Objectives to Be Accomplished

The objectives of evaluation are to rate the teacher's performance. It is assumed that a poor rating will motivate and encourage the teacher to make improvements in his or her performance.

## Activities Conducted

The evaluation process begins with specific judgments about all aspects of the teacher's performance. These judgments are generally the result of one observation.

The next evaluation activity is to prepare a global overview of all of the areas in need of improvement. Little attention is given to the number of areas specified, their levels of difficulty, and the ability of the teacher to manage all of them at once.

The evaluation effort makes the teacher aware of all the limitations of his or her performance. The teacher is then usually provided with a set of suggestions for improvement.

Subjective terms are used when presenting both the areas in need of improvement and the suggestions for their improvement. These subjective terms generally make value judgments about the teacher's performance. Several examples of subjective language follow:

1. *"The students in your class, with few exceptions, are not motivated."*
2. *"The class is inadequately prepared to deal with critical-thinking questions."*
3. *"Your questioning techniques need improvement."*

Some subjective terms in common use are:

| | | |
|---|---|---|
| a strength | outstanding | excellent |
| acceptable | satisfactory | good |
| improvement needed | inadequate | fair |
| unacceptable | unsatisfactory | poor |

## Resulting Outcomes

The outcomes of the evaluation activities are usually both negative and unproductive. Because the evaluation activities create teacher demoralization, frustration, and suspicion, they do not help the teacher improve his or her teaching performance.

Evaluation activities create demoralization because few people are motivated by criticism. Heaping a heavy load of areas in need of improvement on the teacher will tend to reduce his or her morale and result in even less effective performance.

The teacher's unsuccessful efforts may be performed with the same sincere intent as successful ones. A notification of failure is frustrating and tends to make people give up.

The judgmental aspect of evaluation cultivates an adversary relationship. The teacher becomes suspicious that he or she will be hurt rather than helped by the experience.

## SUM UP YOUR SUPERVISORY EFFORTS WITH YOUR TEACHERS

It is, of course, important to bring closure to your supervisory efforts at the end of the school year. Rather than evaluate the teachers, summarize your own supervisory efforts. This summary serves four purposes:

1. To record those aspects of each teacher's performance that were targeted for improvement
2. To outline the improvement plan implemented
3. To describe the results of the plan implemented
4. To plan supervisory efforts for the following year

Figures 1-2 and 1-3 show sample supervision summaries for two different evaluation periods.

### Figure 1-2

**SAMPLE SUPERVISION SUMMARY**

**Time Frame:** September – October

**Target Area:** Student discipline

**Improvement Plan:** 1. Establish rules of behavior.
2. The students and the teacher cooperatively establish a class code of behavior.
3. Attention is given only to positive behavior.
4. Parents of certain students are called to school for a conference.
5. Communications with particular parents are continued by telephone and letter.

**Results:**
1. Students appear to respect each other.
2. Students raise their hands to answer questions.
3. Students attend to tasks.
4. There is a hum of meaningful activity in the classroom.
5. Friction and negative interaction among students have been reduced.

**Future Supervisory Efforts to Focus on:** Better organization of lessons.

## Time Frame

The length of time estimated for the successful improvement of a target area will vary greatly with both the teacher's skill and the complexity of the area.

**Figure 1-3**

---

### SAMPLE SUPERVISION SUMMARY

**Time Frame:**  November – February

**Target Area:**  Organization of a lesson

**Improvement Plan:** 1. Planned preparation by the teacher:
—Motivation within the students' experience
—Objective stated: What we will learn
—Sequential development of the lesson
—Medial summary: What have we learned so far?
—Continued development
—Final summary: What have we learned?
—Reinforcement practice
—Homework review
—Teacher evaluation of students

**Results:**  1. Improved comprehension by the students.
2. Fewer students who require a second teaching of the concept.
3. Improved completion of homework assignments.
4. Improved test results.

**Future Supervisory Efforts to Focus on:**  Development of questions at the critical-thinking level.

---

## Target Area

The selection of a particular target area should be the result of diagnosed needs. When several needs have been diagnosed, areas of crucial importance should, of course, be worked on first. However, it may be important to give teachers a sense of accomplishment by working first on areas they can master easily.

## Improvement Plans

The specified improvement plans will reflect the needs and skills of individual teachers in particular areas targeted for improvement. These plans may include:

1. Allocation of resources

2. Visits between colleagues

3. Modeling of appropriate techniques by the supervisor

4. Involvement of additional adults in the classroom

5. Teacher planning with the supervisor

6. Working with district support staff

## Results

Results should be noted in objective terms. Both positive and negative results should be noted. Target-area improvement plans that do not have positive results may be reintroduced or postponed, then worked on later in the year.

## Future Supervisory Efforts

Future plans should reflect other areas that could be improved, but were not the first priority for this school year. Future plans should be reviewed at the start of the new school year and considered in light of new priorities.

# INVOLVE THE TEACHERS IN THE SUPERVISION SUMMARY

The supervision summary (see Figure 1-4) should be prepared in consultation with the teacher. There should be agreement on all aspects of the summary. If possible, the teacher should be the one to identify future areas to be targeted. This involvement helps to motivate teacher efforts.

The supervision summary should be signed by both you and the teacher. Both parties have then agreed to what was done, the specific results, and details about what is still to be done.

# HOW TO TAME THE EVALUATION MONSTER

Despite the negative effects of evaluation, there are at least two good reasons to conduct an evaluation:

1. The district requires an end-of-year rating for each teacher.

2. The district requires the use of a particular evaluation form.

**Figure 1-4**

---

**School Heading**

**SUPERVISION SUMMARY**

Teacher _____ Year Ending _____

Time Frame _____

Target Area _____

_____

Improvement Plan: _____

_____

_____

_____

_____

_____

_____

_____

_____

Results: _____

_____

_____

_____

_____

_____

Future Supervisory Efforts: _____

_____

_____

_____

_____

_____

_____        _____

**Teacher's Signature**                        **Supervisor's Signature**

---

When the use of evaluation as a rating of teachers is required, several strategies will help tame the evaluation monster.

## Involve the Teacher

Invite the teacher to participate in completing the form required by the district. The teacher's input provides his or her professional opinion about the specific areas of performance that are detailed on the form.

In addition, the involvement of the teacher will help to establish a trust relationship and the belief that the supervisor does care about the teacher's concerns.

## Collaboratively Agree on the Rating

When the teacher is involved in the decision about the rating, the teacher is able to participate in a judgment about his or her own effectiveness. This provides an opportunity for the teacher's subjective judgment to be discussed. It also provides an opportunity for open discussion. If improvement of the teacher's performance is the goal, compromising over the rating in order to achieve improved teacher efforts is a course worth considering.

## Form an Action Plan Together

This is the time to secure the teacher's commitment. Specify a plan that will be implemented. Be sure to have the teacher sign the action plan, then put it into effect at the first opportunity.

# Establishing Standard Skills for All Teachers

A description of standard skills for all teachers is helpful in several ways. It provides you with a categorized breakdown of all aspects of the teacher's role. A description of standard skills may, therefore, be used as a guide to specifically direct ongoing supervisory assistance over an extended period of time. It may also be useful in informing teachers of all the aspects of their role, and in focusing the attention of individual teachers on some specific areas.

The following description of standard skills for all teachers is, nonetheless, presented with caution. It is not intended to be used as an observation checklist; it is not practical or helpful to try to observe all aspects of the teacher's role during one observation.

In addition, the description of standard skills should not be used as a skills mastery checklist. Teacher mastery of specific skills may not be consistent. For example, some teachers may organize subject matter perfectly for slow students. That same organization may be deadly for higher achieving groups. As another example, the high energy level some teachers demonstrate at the start of the school year may drop off before holidays, just when students need even greater motivation.

The standard skills for all teachers are divided into six areas:

Classroom Environment
Preparation for Instruction
Interaction With Students
Management of the Learning Environment
Professionalism
Parent/Community Interaction

# CLASSROOM ENVIRONMENT

Anyone who has ever taught knows how important the environment in the classroom is to learning. In order to help your teachers be as effective as possible, you should establish certain standards to ensure that a proper classroom environment is maintained.

## Physical Arrangement of the Room

The physical arrangement and appearance of the classroom are important points to consider when establishing standards for teachers. The furniture should be arranged to provide easy and safe movement of students. Aisles and passageways should be kept clear, entrances and exits kept open, and frequently used areas should be accessible.

The furniture should also be arranged to match the teacher's instructional objectives. This includes seeing to it that all students are able to see the chalkboard, that the teacher can work with individual students when appropriate, that project construction areas are available, and that multi-media is placed and used effectively.

Another important item is the neatness and cleanliness of the classroom. Waste materials should be appropriately discarded, clothing neatly put away, and the floors cleanly swept. The chalkboard and bulletin boards should also be easy to read.

## Arrangement of Materials

The arrangement, display, and appearance of learning materials are also important. These materials should be neatly arranged, organized, and easily available to students. The room displays should reflect current student work.

## Classroom Atmosphere

A crucial element, the atmosphere of the classroom is more difficult to describe. However, you should be able to see evidence of students' ideas being accepted. That is, the students express themselves freely and ask questions. They ask for help and also listen to each other.

In this learning atmosphere, the teacher's physical appearance should be positive. Facial expression and body language are accepting of student needs and the speaking voice is clear—easy to hear and to understand. The teacher's physical vitality demonstrates involvement, energy, and interest in the teaching role.

# PREPARATION FOR INSTRUCTION

To best encourage students to learn, certain standards are recommended for teachers to follow as they prepare their instructional plans. A detailed list of these standards is included here.

## Determination of Student Needs

The teacher who effectively prepares for instruction begins with a determination of student needs. This determination provides both for students who are advanced beyond the current topic as well as for students who are missing skills required by the current topic.

**Student Needs Are Diagnosed.** Students are individually assessed to identify new skills needs and inadequate mastery of skills previously taught.

**Progress Is Monitored.** The needs assessment is ongoing, with continuous monitoring of the students' progress. Attention is given to the needs of individual students and to the group.

## Organization of Subject Matter

After determining student needs, the teacher must organize the subject matter so that instruction is sequential, developmental, and appropriate to all the students in that class.

**The Specified Curriculum Is Taught.** The teacher relates what is taught to the grade's mandated curriculum in each subject area.

**Content Presentation Is Sequential.** The sequence in which skills and concepts are presented is appropriate to both the material and the levels of ability of the students.

## Instructional Plan

A specific and detailed plan for instruction contributes to efficient and effective delivery to students. The teacher's planning for instruction takes into consideration time allocation, differences among students, skill needs, and the possibility of teacher absence.

**Time Is Appropriately Allocated.** The teacher sets realistic time frames for completion of the task, depending upon the ability of the students, the individual needs of particular students, and the difficulty of the material.

**Individual Differences Are Addressed.** The teacher keeps in mind that slow and fast students may study the same topic but in vastly different ways. Fast students may learn the basic concepts quickly and then explore the subject in depth, use the information to create an original project, and then go on to a new topic. Slower students will need practice, review, and reinforcement experiences.

**Skill Gaps Are Addressed.** The teacher provides instruction for individual students who have not mastered previously taught skills.

**Provision Is Made for Teacher Absence.** Lesson plans include activities that could be conducted by a substitute teacher. This will prevent loss of valuable instructional time.

## Effective Use of Resources

Good planning provides for using the most effective resources available. Following are some of the teacher considerations in this area.

**Provides for Variety in Instruction.** The teacher identifies appropriate resources and brings them to the classroom. Subject matter is clarified, reinforced, and made more exciting through the use of all types of representative materials.

**Considers Individual Learning Styles.** The teacher provides resources suited to the preferences of students who are oral, visual, tactile, and kinesthetic learners.

**Seeks Outside Resources.** The teacher uses outside resources, such as the public library, teacher centers, class trips, and people from the community, to enrich the learning experience.

**Operates Equipment Effectively and Safely.** Machines needed for the presentation of materials are appropriately placed, operated with care, turned off when not in use, and returned when no longer needed.

# INTERACTION WITH STUDENTS

A teacher's ability to interact effectively with students is one of the most important skills he or she can hone. While it is impossible to catalog all of these skills, many can be addressed by the supervisor.

## Effective Use of Student Responses

How students' responses are used, valued, clarified, used for summary, and directed when incorrect often determines whether a student learns or is turned off in the classroom.

**Responses Are Valued.** The individual student's response is repeated by the teacher, the student, or another student because it is important.

**Responses Are Clarified.** The teacher paraphrases individual student responses or modifies them to make them better understood. The original idea of the student's response, is, however, kept intact.

**Responses Are Related and Extended.** The teacher uses the student's response as an example of a situation, an explanation of an idea, or a comparison with something else that has been discussed. Whenever possible, the teacher uses the students' responses rather than his or her own words.

**Responses Are Used to Summarize.** The teacher uses the students' responses to draw a conclusion, make a point, or summarize the concept taught.

**Deals with Incorrect Responses.** Students are motivated to participate when they believe they can give a wrong answer without penalty. When an incorrect answer is given, the teacher states the question for which the student's answer would have been correct, states the situation that would make the answer correct, rephrases the question, provides additional information, and probes the student's response.

## Variety of Questions Asked

Questioning is a second crucial area of teacher-student interaction. The skill with which the teacher uses a variety of questions of low, high, and open types usually reflects the teacher's effectiveness.

**Lower-Level Questions.** Lower-level questions provide the basis for knowledge and understanding, according to Bloom's Taxonomy. Such questions use verbs like tell, define, identify, list, name, explain, describe. Questions at this level provide the foundation of information to use for thinking on higher levels.

**Higher-Level Questions.** Higher-level questions provide for analysis, synthesis, and evaluation thinking, according to Bloom's Taxonomy. Such questions use verbs like categorize, classify, compare, change, design, develop, invent, modify, argue, judge, predict, recommend.

**Open Questions.** These are questions that do not require merely a "yes" or "no" answer, or a one-word answer. Open questions encourage students to express themselves in full sentences.

## Using Motivation Techniques

All learning begins with motivation, and an important standard skill for all teachers is the use of student experience to bridge the gap between what is known and the unfamiliar. In addition, students' learning improves when they are aware of specifically what is to be taught in the lesson.

**Uses Student Experiences.** The teacher relates new information to past experiences that most students have in common. For example, the teacher might ask, "What is the first resource you would turn to when dealing with a problem?"

**Uses Past Knowledge.** As a means of building a bridge from the known to the unknown, the teacher relates new information to previous lessons taught. For example, the teacher might ask, "What are some of the ways we have discussed in which people provide for their needs?" "What would happen if the forests were burned?"

**Clarifies Importance.** The teacher makes students aware of what they are to learn and how that knowledge is of importance to them.

## Variety of Instructional Approaches Used

The use of a variety of instructional approaches serves to make teachers more effective in their interaction with students and, therefore, improves the teaching-learning process.

**Lecture.** The teacher instructs students in a sequential and developmental manner. Students are expected to listen attentively.

**Discussion.** The teacher presents statements and questions to students, who are expected to react, compare, value, and judge.

**Hands-on Involvement of Students.** The teacher provides materials to students, who are expected to manipulate, change, use, or build with the materials.

**Independent Work.** The teacher presents students with objectives, materials, and a time frame. They are expected to use the materials within the given time frame to reach the stated objectives on their own or with a minimum of assistance from the teacher.

## Variety of Instructional Groups Attempted

Variety in instructional grouping contributes to teachers' interacting more effectively with students because it adds interest to the lesson content and helps students learn from and relate to other students, as well as to the teacher.

**Whole Class.** The teacher presents, to the whole class, a concept or skill that all of the children have not yet mastered.

**Groups.** The teacher presents a concept or skill to a group of students who are ready for that instruction, who need a second teaching of that skill or concept, or who require additional information or instruction. The instructional content is not appropriate to the whole class.

**One-to-One.** The teacher presents a concept or skill to one student who is ready for that instruction, who needs a second teaching of that skill or concept, or who requires additional information or instruction. The instructional content is appropriate only to the individual student.

**Peer Instruction.** Two students work together in an instructional pairing to learn from each other, or one student helps the other to learn.

**Self-Directed.** The individual student works on his or her own to learn, reinforce, apply, or enrich the understanding of a concept or skill.

# MANAGEMENT OF THE LEARNING ENVIRONMENT

Some teachers are born masters at managing the learning environment. The teaching effectiveness of those who are not can be improved dramatically if they are made aware of specific areas of classroom management on which to concentrate. The following section helps you pinpoint some of these areas.

## Recordkeeping

Successful classrooms are made or broken by the management skills of the teacher. An important feature of a successful classroom, therefore, is the keeping of accurate records.

**Daily Interaction.** The teacher records notes and evaluations of daily contact with individuals and groups, noting how particular students perform in class.

**Participation in Classroom Activities.** The teacher records notes and evaluations about the individual student's completion of classroom assignments.

**Completion of Homework.** The teacher records notes and evaluations about the individual student's completion of homework assignments.

**Production of Products.** The teacher records notes and evaluations about the individual projects that are completed by each student.

**Test Results.** The teacher records notes and evaluations about the test scores of individual students following an assessment of particular skills. The notes include an identification of skill needs and areas of nonmastery.

## Established Routines

Another important aspect of a successful classroom is the establishment of routines, which are maintained and effectively used by the students.

**Use of the Classroom.** Teacher and students agree upon specific rules about how the classroom should be used. Procedures for using, locating, and returning materials are set, and students are aware of when, how, and where to use particular resources.

**Leaving/Entering the Classroom.** Teacher and students agree upon specific rules about how to enter and leave the classroom.

**Completing Work.** Teacher and students agree upon specific rules about where, how, and when work is to be completed. Specific procedures for collecting and returning work are also established.

## Discipline Guidelines

Classrooms having the right kind of atmosphere for successful teaching and learning display certain characteristics. These necessary characteristics include the following:

**Noise Is Controlled.** The classroom is a busy and meaningful environment in which noise is appropriate to the activity in process. The students' learning opportunities are not hindered by excessive noise or by limitations on discussion.

**Complaints Are Dealt With.** The teacher recognizes and deals effectively with students' complaints and makes an appropriate decision about what action or inaction to take to satisfy the complaint.

**Student Friction Is Controlled.** The teacher recognizes and deals effectively with friction between students. The teacher then takes effective action to eliminate the friction and prevent its return.

**Students Respond to a Request for Order.**  Students know how a request for order will be made, and they repond immediately to that request.

**Students Pay Attention to the Lesson.**  During a teacher-directed lesson, students are involved and attentive. Students not involved in the lesson are meaningfully and quietly involved in other assignments.

# PROFESSIONALISM

The degree of professionalism that teachers demonstrate marks the difference between the good teacher and the great teacher. To the great teacher, the art of teaching is not a job, but rather a career, a dedication, a profession.

## Relationship With Colleagues

Professionalism is demonstrated by the teacher's cordial and helpful relationships with colleagues.

**Cordial and Friendly Interaction Exists.** Relationships with other teachers and with supervisors are cordial and friendly. The teacher greets others in a friendly manner and engages them in conversations.

**Helpful and Encouraging Interaction Exists.** The teacher responds positively to requests from staff members and encourages the efforts of peers.

## Self-Development

Interest and involvement in self-development is another characteristic of the teacher's professionalism.

**Stays Current With the Field.** The teacher is knowledgeable about current theory and practice from reading educational journals and magazines, and attending conferences.

**Involved in Staff Development Activities.** The teacher learns new techniques and approaches by participating in in-service and/or university course work.

**Seeks and Shares Ideas/Information.** The teacher asks about the techniques and activities of colleagues and shares his or her own ideas and information on educational subjects. The teacher agrees to participate in or to present new approaches.

**Committee Involvement.** The teacher participates in committees seeking to evaluate and/or prepare approaches, suggestions, or techniques.

**Engages in Self-Evaluation.** The teacher is interested in and participates in ongoing self-evaluation of his or her effectiveness with a peer, supervisor, or alone.

## School Policy

Professionalism is also reflected in the teacher's involvement with the development, improvement, and practice of school policies.

**Aware of Procedures.** The teacher is aware of procedures and practices in current use by the school.

**Follows Guidelines.** The teacher follows the policies and procedures that are in effect. When it becomes impossible or impractical to follow procedure, the teacher discusses the problem with a supervisor.

**Participates in Evaluation.** The teacher participates in the evaluation of school policy by offering practical input about how the policy is working and how to make it more effective and efficient.

**Participates in the Development of New Policy.** When necessary, the teacher becomes involved in the identification of problems and the development of new policy.

# PARENT/COMMUNITY INTERACTION

The teacher's interaction with parents and the community contributes greatly to the success of both the individual teacher and the school. The value of the school and the esteem in which it is held by the community are often the result of teacher interactions.

## Holds Conferences With Individual Parents

An important consideration of effective parent/community interaction is the teacher's attitude during conferences.

**Is Available.** The teacher makes him- or herself available to parents. At times, conferences with parents may be held before school, after school, or during evening hours. The teacher should call parents during the evening hours when necessary.

**Is Interested.** During interactions with parents, the teacher maintains an interested attitude about all of the factors that affect the student's performance in school.

**Is Helpful.** The teacher offers suggestions for improving the current situation. These suggestions may involve efforts on the part of both the teacher and the parent.

**Is Confidential.** All matters discussed with parents are kept confidential. The teacher does not involve him- or herself in idle gossip. Information is shared only when and with whom it should be shared for the best interests of the student.

## Interprets Educational Information

A teacher's desire and effectiveness in interpreting educational information is another aspect of the standard for successful teaching.

**Test Results.** The teacher explains the items evaluated, the scores achieved, and the standing of the student. The teacher compares the student's progress with former achievements of *that* student, never with classmates.

**Student Involvement in Particular Programs.** The teacher discusses and explains to the parents the particular programs in which the student is involved. The teacher discusses why the student was involved, how the program will be of benefit, what results may be expected, and how those results will be reported to the parents.

## Encourages Parent/Community Involvement

A final consideration is the degree to which the teacher encourages and values parent and community involvement.

**Invites Parents to Visit.** The teacher encourages parents and members of the community to visit the classroom to observe, firsthand, how the student works and behaves and how the programs operate.

**Seeks Community Interaction.** The teacher requests participation from various parts of the community to enrich and enlarge the instructional resources available to students.

**Supports Community Efforts.** The teacher actively participates in community efforts and encourages others to participate. The teacher is sympathetic to community needs and aspirations.

Figure 2-1 shows a summary outline of standard skills for all teachers. Remember that the description of standard skills is intended to:

1. Provide the supervisor with a categorized breakdown of all the aspects of the teacher's role.
2. Be used as a guide to specifically direct ongoing supervisory assistance over an extended period of time.
3. Inform teachers of all the aspects of their role.
4. Focus the attention of individual teachers on specific areas.

The summary outline (see Figure 2-1) is *not* intended to be used as an observation checklist or serve as a skills mastery checklist.

**Figure 2-1**

## OUTLINE OF STANDARD SKILLS

| AREAS AND COMPONENTS | SPECIFICS |
|---|---|
| **CLASSROOM ENVIRONMENT** | |
| Physical Arrangement | 1. Furniture is arranged to provide easy and safe movement of students.<br>2. Furniture is arranged to match instructional objectives.<br>3. The classroom is neat and clean. |
| Materials Arrangement | 1. Learning materials are organized, easily available, and neat.<br>2. Room displays reflect current student work. |
| Atmosphere | 1. Student ideas are accepted.<br>2. Teacher's physical appearance is positive. |
| **PREPARATION FOR INSTRUCTION** | |
| Determination of Needs | 1. Student needs are diagnosed.<br>2. Students are individually assessed.<br>3. Progress is monitored. |
| Organization of Subject Matter | 1. The specified curriculum is taught.<br>2. Content presentation is sequential. |
| Instructional Plan | 1. Time is appropriately allocated.<br>2. Individual differences are addressed.<br>3. Skill gaps are addressed.<br>4. Provision is made for teacher absence. |
| Use of Resources | 1. Provides for variety in instruction.<br>2. Considers individual learning styles.<br>3. Seeks outside resources.<br>4. Operates equipment effectively and safely. |
| **INTERACTION WITH STUDENTS** | |
| Use of Student Responses | 1. Responses are valued.<br>2. Responses are clarified.<br>3. Responses are related and extended.<br>4. Responses are used to summarize.<br>5. Deals with incorrect responses. |
| Types of Questions Asked | 1. Lower-level questions.<br>2. Higher-level questions.<br>3. Open questions. |
| Motivation Techniques | 1. Uses student experiences.<br>2. Uses past knowledge.<br>3. Clarifies importance. |
| Variety of Instructional Approaches | 1. Lecture.<br>2. Discussion.<br>3. Hands-on involvement.<br>4. Independent work. |

## Figure 2-1 (continued)

| Variety of Instructional Groups | 1. Whole class. |
|---|---|
| | 2. Groups. |
| | 3. One-to-one. |
| | 4. Peer instruction. |
| | 5. Self-directed. |

### MANAGEMENT OF THE LEARNING ENVIRONMENT

| Recordkeeping | 1. Daily interaction. |
|---|---|
| | 2. Participation in classroom activities. |
| | 3. Completion of homework. |
| | 4. Production of products. |
| | 5. Test results. |

| Established Routines | 1. Use of the classroom. |
|---|---|
| | 2. Leaving/entering the classroom. |
| | 3. Completing work. |

| Discipline Guidelines | 1. Noise control. |
|---|---|
| | 2. Deals with complaints. |
| | 3. Controls student friction. |
| | 4. Students respond to a request for order. |
| | 5. Students attentive to the lesson. |

### PROFESSIONALISM

| Relationship With Colleagues | 1. Cordial and friendly interaction. |
|---|---|
| | 2. Helpful and encouraging interaction. |

| Self-Development | 1. Stays current with the field. |
|---|---|
| | 2. Involved in staff development activities. |
| | 3. Seeks and shares ideas/information. |
| | 4. Committee involvement. |
| | 5. Engages in self-evaluation. |

| School Policy | 1. Aware of procedures. |
|---|---|
| | 2. Follows guidelines. |
| | 3. Participates in evaluation. |
| | 4. Participates in the development of new policy. |

### PARENT/COMMUNITY INTERACTION

| Holds Conferences With Individual Parents | 1. Is available. |
|---|---|
| | 2. Is interested. |
| | 3. Is helpful. |
| | 4. Is confidential. |

| Interprets Educational Information | 1. Test results. |
|---|---|
| | 2. Student involvement in particular programs. |

| Encourages Involvement | 1. Invites parents to visit. |
|---|---|
| | 2. Seeks community interaction. |
| | 3. Supports community efforts. |

# Making Pull-Out Programs Effective

Standard skills necessary for all teachers apply, of course, to teachers of pull-out programs. These programs are both a blessing and a curse because, although they provide specialized services to selected students, they remove those students from the regular class during the instructional day. Therefore, pull-out programs create problems that require special consideration and control by the supervisor. This can be done by establishing solution strategies and then monitoring those strategies to ensure they are ongoing, of high quality, and effective.

## TAILORING SCHEDULES TO MEET EVERYONE'S NEEDS

### Problem One

• Students in pull-out programs miss classwork that continues while they are out of the classroom.

### Solution Strategies

1. Individual students are usually involved in only one pull-out program. It is therefore possible to

**25**

schedule all pull-out programs for each grade at the same time period. Students in programs for remediation, English second language, special education, and so forth, would leave and return at the same time. The class teacher is usually left with a smaller group of on- and above-level students, so that the time could be used for special instruction either individually or in a group. Planning a common pull-out time period for the grade usually provides a sufficient number of students for each pull-out program.

2. When a common pull-out time frame is not practical, helping teachers plot possible instructional time may be an alternative. By plotting which students, and therefore which reading and mathematics groups, are not in perfect attendance the teacher can plan to instruct complete groups at any given time. This also helps the teacher determine when and for how long the entire class is available for instruction, conferences, or progress checks. Figure 3-1 shows a sample plot for possible instructional time.

3. When a departmental program is used, it may be possible to schedule pull-out programs during related subject time. For example, English second language students may be scheduled during foreign language instruction periods. Or the time periods for study hall, some minor subjects, or clubs may have to be used. Students involved in programs for the gifted may have to make choices among several school programs such as band, chorus, clubs, and the like.

## Problem Two

- Individuals and small groups of students move through the halls at all times of the day.

## Solution Strategies

1. If possible, pull-out program teachers should pick up and return their students, thus ensuring that all youngsters are supervised. This strategy also helps prevent late arrival or nonattendance because the student was not aware of the time. The pickup and return procedure will probably not be difficult for the pull-out teacher since classes on the same grade are usually clustered in the same part of the building. The time lost in pickup and return of the students is more than made up by consistent attendance and punctuality.

2. If students must go unescorted to pull-out program rooms, they should carry a pass or program card that states why they are in the halls and where they are going.

3. Pull-out program teachers can prevent lateness and nonattendance by submitting a student lateness or nonattendance report to the class teacher when appropriate. The class teacher's response to the report helps both teachers deal with problem students. A sample lateness/nonattendance report is shown in Figure 3-2.

## Figure 3-1

| | | | | | | |
|---|---|---|---|---|---|---|
| **POSSIBLE INSTRUCTIONAL TIME** | | | | | | |
| **TIME** | **O/A*** | **MON** | **TUES** | **WED** | **THURS** | **FRI** |
| 9-9:30 | O | Juan(R1, M2) Mary(R2, M1) | NONE | Juan(R1, M2) Mary(R2, M1) | NONE | Juan(R1, M2) Mary(R2, M1) |
| | A | Read Gp 3 Math Gp 3 | ALL | Read Gp 3 Math Gp 3 | ALL | Read Gp 3 Math Gp 3 |
| 9:30-10 | O | Tom(R3, M1) | Tom(R3, M1) | Tom(R3, M1) | Tom(R3, M1) | Tom(R3, M1) |
| | A | Read Gp 1,2 Math Gp 2,3 | Read Gp 1,2 Math Gp 2,3 | Read Gp 1,2 Math Gp 2,3 | Read Gp 1,2 Math Gp 2,3 | Read Gp 1,2 Math Gp 2,3 |
| 10-10:30 | O | NONE | NONE | NONE | NONE | NONE |
| | A | Read Gp 1,2,3 Math Gp 1,2,3 | GYM | Read Gp 1,2,3 Math Gp 1,2,3 | GYM | Read Gp 1,2,3 Math Gp 1,2,3 |
| 10:30-11 | O | NONE | NONE | NONE | NONE | NONE |
| | A | MUSIC | Read Gp 1,2,3 Math Gp 1,2,3 | ART | Read Gp 1,2,3 Math Gp 1,2,3 | CLASS |
| 11-11:30 | O | Marie(R1, M1) | Marie(R1, M1) | Marie(R1, M1) | Marie(R1, M1) | Marie(R1, M1) |
| | A | Read Gp 2,3 Math Gp 2,3 | Read Gp 2,3 Math Gp 2,3 | Read Gp 2,3 Math Gp 2,3 | Read Gp 2,3 Math Gp 2,3 | Read Gp 2,3 Math Gp 2,3 |
| 11:30-12 | O | NONE | NONE | NONE | NONE | NONE |
| | A | ALL | ALL | ALL | ALL | ALL |
| 1-1:30 | O | NONE | NONE | NONE | NONE | NONE |
| | A | Read Gp 1,2,3 Math Gp 1,2,3 | Read Gp 1,2,3 Math Gp 1,2,3 | Read Gp 1,2,3 Math Gp 1,2,3 | Read Gp 1,2,3 Math Gp 1,2,3 | LIBRARY |
| 1:30-2 | O | NONE | NONE | NONE | NONE | NONE |
| | A | ALL | ALL | ALL | ALL | ALL |
| 2-2:30 | O | Jim(R3, M3) Theresa(R3, M3) | NONE | Jim(R3, M3) Theresa(R3, M3) | NONE | CHORUS |
| | A | Read Gp 1,2 Math Gp 1,2 | ALL | Read Gp 1,2 Math Gp 1,2 | ALL | Individual conferences |
| 2:30-3 | O | Jim(R3, M3) Theresa(R3, M3) | NONE | Jim(R3, M3) Theresa(R3, M3) | NONE | Individual conferences |
| | A | Individual conferences | ALL | Individual conferences | ALL | Individual conferences |

*O = students out of the room
A = groups/class available for instruction
R = reading group
M = mathematics group

Figure 3-2

**MEMO**

To:     **Class Teacher:** _____

From: **Pull-Out Program:** _____

        **Teacher:** _____

Re:     **Lateness/Nonattendance**
        **(circle appropriate one)**

**Student's Name:** _____

**Date:** _____

**Time:** _____

**Number of Past Occurrences:** _____

**CLASS TEACHER'S RESPONSE:**
_____ **I have spoken to the student.**
_____ **We need to confer about this problem.**
_____ **A parent conference is necessary.**
_____ **The principal has been notified.**
_____ **Other** _____

_____

## COMMUNICATING WITH THE CLASSROOM TEACHER ABOUT THE PROGRAM

Problem

- The regular class teacher usually knows little or nothing about the pull-out program.

Solution Strategies

1. Each pull-out program teacher should prepare a written program description that includes the rationale for the program, its relationship to the regular class program, identification of students for the program, types of activities con-

ducted, materials used, the evaluation process, and expected results. The program description should be given to each class teacher in the school.

2. Each teacher of a pull-out program may present the program at a general faculty conference. Classroom teachers should have the opportunity to look through materials in the room where the program is conducted and to participate in some of the activities.

# SETTING DOWN RESPONSIBILITIES OF THE PROGRAM TEACHER AND THE CLASSROOM TEACHER

## Problems

- The classroom teacher usually is not informed about the performance of his or her student in the pull-out program.
- There may be confusion about whether the class teacher or the program teacher is responsible for the student's progress in a particular content area. For example, who is responsible for the reading progress of students in remedial reading programs?
- The individual student is usually assigned homework by both teachers.

## Solution Strategies

1. All three problems can be resolved by establishing a specific time for conferences between the teachers. The specified time will depend upon the individual school's program. Conference periods can be planned during the early morning, as part of the class teacher's preparation periods, during the lunch period, during gym periods, or at times when the class is working on independent assignments. These conferences should occur about once a month.

2. The conferences will help both teachers share information about the student, plan for his or her continued progress, and establish joint responsibility for the student's progress.

3. The pull-out program teacher should bring samples of the student's work to the conference. The class teacher should initial and date the student's work folder after the work has been reviewed.

4. If homework overload is a problem, the teachers should be able to reach a compromise at the conference. They may work out a specific plan to contact each other when special projects are assigned.

5. About once a month, between conferences, the pull-out program teacher should prepare a written report of progress (see Figure 3-3) for the class teacher.

**Figure 3-3**

## PROGRESS REPORT

Program _____

Student _____ Class_____

Date _____

**Objectives Focused on This Month:**

1. _____

   _____

2. _____

   _____

3. _____

   _____

4. _____

   _____

**Activities: (attach student work samples)**

1. _____

2. _____

3. _____

4. _____

**Evaluation: (related to objectives)**

1. _____

2. _____

3. _____

4. _____

**Program Teacher's Signature** _____

This report will keep the class teacher up-to-date about specific objectives and activities currently in progress. Each teacher should keep a copy of the progress reports, which may be of value during the conferences.

# REDUCING HOSTILITY BETWEEN TEACHERS

## Problem

- Regular class teachers may feel hostile toward pull-out program teachers for two reasons: (1) the large difference in the size of the group with which each teacher deals, and (2) the belief that the pull-out program teacher has more prestige.

## Solution Strategies

1. Hopefully, the faculty conference presentation, written program description, monthly progress reports, and conferences will help the class teacher understand that the job of the pull-out program teacher is not an easy one.
2. Hostility may also be reduced by soliciting the class teacher's opinion and suggestions about the needs of the youngster and the instructional strategies that appear to work best.
3. The class teacher may be invited to identify particular areas of difficulty that the student is having with the class curriculum. Specific worksheets, contracts, and homework assignments may be sent to the pull-out teacher with a request that the student be given help in completing them.

# COMMUNICATING WITH PARENTS

## Problem

- Parents are generally uninformed about the pull-out programs and their relationship to the students.

## Solution Strategies

1. General parent information meetings can be planned. At this time, pull-out program teachers can introduce the programs and discuss their purposes and practices.
2. Parents should be invited to conferences with pull-out program teachers to discuss the progress of their youngsters in the program.

3. A pull-out program progress report (see Figure 3-4) should be included with the regular report card sent to parents. This report may include a summary cover sheet with copies of the appropriate monthly progress reports, sent to the class teacher, attached.

## Figure 3-4

**SCHOOL HEADING**

**PROGRESS REPORT TO PARENTS**

Special Program _____

Teacher _____

Student _____

Key: E = Excellent      G = Good      F = Fair      U = Unsatisfactory

**REPORT PERIODS**

|  | 1 | 2 | 3 | 4 |
|---|---|---|---|---|
| Student Attitude |  |  |  |  |
| Completion of Work |  |  |  |  |
| Progress |  |  |  |  |

Monthly progress reports are attached.

Parent's Signature: Period 1. _____

2. _____

3. _____

4. _____

# USING LIMITED TIME EFFECTIVELY

Problem

• The student generally spends a short period of time with the pull-out program teacher, usually forty-five minutes per day.

## Solution Strategies

1. The pull-out program teacher must do meticulous planning throughout the year to make effective use of limited time.

2. The pull-out program teacher must state specific objectives for individual students in Public Law 94-142 programs, or groups of students in remediation, English second language, and so forth. The objectives must be related to student activities, homework assigned, and evaluation of student efforts. Figure 3-5 shows a sample plan for a student in a pull-out program related to Public Law 94-142. Figure 3-6 shows a plan for students in an English second language program.

### Figure 3-5

---

**SAMPLE PLAN FOR STUDENT IN
PULL-OUT PROGRAM RELATED TO PUBLIC LAW 94-142**

**Student** _____ Julie Harrison _____  **Date** _week of March 3_

**Objective** _Individual Educational Plan_____

       **Develop** 1. auditory memory_____

                2. expressive language_____

                3. reading comprehension_____

**Activities Related to Objectives:**

1. Listen to a tape of a fable. After listening, Julie will record five facts learned. She will discuss the facts learned and the meaning of the fable with the teacher.

2. Julie will tell the other students in the group about the fable she has listened to. She will explain what happened in the story and why these actions took place. She will answer the questions of the other students.

3. Julie will read the social studies chapter assigned by the class teacher. She will answer questions related to the text. The teacher will review the questions with Julie and refer to sections in the text when necessary.

---

**Figure 3-6**

---

**SAMPLE PLAN FOR STUDENTS IN
AN ENGLISH SECOND LANGUAGE PROGRAM**

**Group** _New arrivals with little or no English_   **Date** _week of April 1_

**Objectives** 1. to learn the names of people and common objects

2. to use verbs related to immediate action

3. to use speech patterns in conversation

**Activities Related to Objectives:**

1. Students will practice identifying an object with its name, such as book, window, boy, girl, teacher.
2. Students will practice using verbs related to actions, such as the boy goes to school, the teacher sees the girl, the children go home.
3. Students will practice speech patterns in conversation, such as "I am a boy (girl). My name is _____. I live in _____. I go to school. I have _____ brothers (sisters)."

---

## SUPERVISING THE PULL-OUT PROGRAM

Administrators should supervise the pull-out programs to ensure that they are ongoing, are offering quality instruction, and are effective. Supervisors can do this by:

1. Reading the plans of the pull-out program teachers.
2. Requesting classroom teachers to include with their plans the monthly progress reports of students in pull-out programs and the lateness/nonattendance memos.
3. Reviewing the reports to parents before they are sent home.
4. Informally visiting the classrooms of pull-out teachers.
5. Holding conferences with pull-out teachers.
6. Holding conferences with class teachers about the pull-out programs.
7. Walking through the halls during change-of-period times.
8. Reproducing and distributing teacher descriptions of the pull-out programs.
9. Planning and implementing faculty conferences on pull-out programs.
10. Conducting parent meetings on the subject of pull-out programs.

# Categorizing Teacher Types

Administrators are aware that there are differences in effectiveness among teachers on their staff. These differences exist even among those teachers believed to be excellent. The differences among teachers can be pinpointed by identifying the strengths and needs of individuals in three distinct areas of effectiveness:

1. Level of personal involvement
2. Ability to analyze and solve problems
3. Level of teaching skill

## LEVEL OF PERSONAL INVOLVEMENT IN TEACHING

Personal involvement of the teacher involves motivation, enthusiasm, high energy, commitment to the job, and concern for students. Each of these components is described more fully in this section.

### Motivation/Enthusiasm for the Profession

This is the excitement and interest the teacher has in his or her professional role. It is the degree to which the teacher believes that teaching is a proud and important life's work.

### High Energy Level

This is the interest the teacher has in putting forth a wholehearted effort. It is the teacher's willingness to expend energy when working with students, as well as the total physical, mental, and emotional involvement.

### Time Commitment to the Job

This is the amount of time that the teacher is willing to give to his or her role as teacher. It is the teacher's desire to come to school early and stay late to complete work or do a better job; the teacher's attendance at late afternoon or evening meetings; and the teacher's desire to speak to parents even if the phone call must be made during evening hours.

### Professional Concerns

This is the degree of concern that the teacher demonstrates about his or her students. It is the teacher's concern with the personal development of skills and abilities related to the profession of teaching, and the teacher's desire to become involved with problems relating to school concerns or with the problems of other staff members.

The level of personal involvement varies greatly among teachers. Some teachers demonstrate a high degree of personal involvement, while others have a very low degree or a moderate degree. Figure 4-1 gives examples of teacher behavior in each degree of involvement.

## ABILITY TO ANALYZE AND SOLVE PROBLEMS

In order to analyze and solve problems, a teacher must have the ability to:

1. Identify the problem
2. Analyze the situation
3. Propose solutions
4. Develop a plan

## Figure 4-1

### LEVEL OF PERSONAL INVOLVEMENT

| Aspects | High Degree | Moderate Degree | Low Degree |
|---|---|---|---|
| Motivation/ Enthusiasm | excited | interested | bored |
| Energy Level | moves around the room; actively involved with students; sits with students on chairs or on the floor | walks among the students; watches students involved in work; sits next to students | stays at the front of the room; reads or does other work while students are involved with work; sits alone and calls students to his or her desk |
| Time Commitment | comes early, leaves late; attends after-school and evening meetings; calls parents in the evening | usually comes early, sometimes leaves late; attends some afternoon meetings | sometimes arrives late, leaves punc-tually; does not attend many meet-ings or arrives late |
| Concern for: students | works with groups, individuals, special teachers, counselors, and parents | works with groups, individuals, and parents | works with groups |
| self | reads journals; attends courses; discusses ideas | attends courses; discusses ideas | knows the teacher's contract |
| others | demonstrates for other teachers; shares materials with other teachers; offers to prepare materials for others | shares materials that are requested by others | |
| school | joins committees; volunteers | serves on committees when asked | |

### Identify the Problem

This is the teacher's ability to sense or identify that something is wrong or that something could be better. It is the ability to know when something is not as good as it might be, and the desire to make even what is good a little better.

### Analyze the Situation

This is the ability of the teacher to examine all aspects of the situation to determine what parts are not running smoothly and then to make efforts to find the trouble spots.

### Propose Solutions

This is the teacher's ability to propose a variety of possible solutions, ideas, or suggestions for solving the problem. The focus is on finding, not just one, but many different alternative solutions to consider.

### Develop a Plan

This is the teacher's ability to select the best possible solution from among all the ideas and suggestions explored. The solution is then incorporated into a well-thought-out plan of action, and the plan is implemented.

As with personal involvement, the ability to analyze and solve problems varies among teachers. This area of teacher effectiveness is perhaps the most individual of all. Even excellent teachers with a high degree of personal involvement and good teaching skills do not always have a well-developed ability to analyze problems. This ability is found in intuitive, insightful, and analytical people. However, it is possible to help teachers develop the ability. Figure 4-2 gives examples of teacher behavior in each degree of the ability to analyze and solve problems.

## LEVEL OF TEACHING SKILL

A teacher's level of teaching skill is critical to his or her performance and to student learning.

**Figure 4-2**

**ABILITY TO ANALYZE AND SOLVE PROBLEMS**

| Aspects | High Degree | Moderate Degree | Low Degree |
|---|---|---|---|
| Identify the Problem | seeks improvement; personally identifies problems | agrees with identification if told about it | unaware of problem; does not agree if told about it |
| Analyze the Situation | examines the problem; sees different sides of the problem; sees why and what the problem is about | examines the problem; sees only one aspect of the problem; sees what the problem is but not why the problem developed | confused about the problem; cannot see the parts of the whole |
| Propose Solutions | develops many solution ideas | develops one or two solution ideas | has no ideas; gives up |
| Develop a Plan | can select the one best solution idea; creates a step-by-step plan for implementation | can select the one best solution idea; cannot prepare a solution plan | "tell me" "show me" |

## Instructional Approaches

Considered here is the teacher's ability to diagnose student needs and to appropriately prescribe for them. The teacher must be able to use a variety of instructional presentations, including lecture, discussion, instructional groups, peer-to-peer instruction, and one-to-one teacher instruction. The teacher must also be able to instruct in ways that are creative, motivating, and effective, such as linking new knowledge to the past experiences and information of the students, and asking appropriate questions.

## Selection of Materials

This is the teacher's awareness of the variety of types of materials that appeal to and are effective with students, including materials that are appropriate for oral, visual, tactile, and kinesthetic learners. Also included is the interest of the teacher in searching for new and exciting materials for the students, as well as the teacher's ability to use materials in the most effective ways.

## Management Ability

This is the ability of the teacher to establish an organized and effective classroom environment, to keep high quality and accurate records, and to group and regroup students for instruction. It is also the teacher's ability to eliminate harmful noise and disorder from the classroom and to maintain control over a variety of activities.

The level of teaching skill is usually directly related to the amount of teaching experience a teacher has had. Generally, more experienced teachers organize and manage all aspects of the classroom better than do new and inexperienced teachers. There are, unfortunately, some experienced teachers who have problems maintaining order and discipline or keeping records or involving students through good questioning techniques. Figure 4-3 gives examples of teacher behavior in each degree of teaching skill.

# MATCHING TEACHER TYPE TO SUPERVISORY LEVEL OF CONTROL

Supervisors can identify teacher strengths and needs by analyzing the degree of their performance in each area of teaching effectiveness. Assess each teacher individually. As you conduct the diagnostic activities described in Part II, check the teacher's degree of performance for each aspect of the three areas of teaching effectiveness. (See Figure 4-4 on page 42.) The resulting analysis will be helpful in two ways:

1. It will help you pinpoint specific teacher strengths and needs. Supervisory help can then be most effective.

2. It will help you decide the amount of control you wish to use in working with each teacher. Teachers at a high degree of performance and teachers at a low degree of performance require very different involvement with the supervisor.

Analyze the results of each teacher's "Level of Effectiveness Assessment." Determine where each teacher is checked on various aspects of the three areas of teaching effectiveness—high, moderate, or low degree. Then, by categorizing the teacher type, you can select the level of control that is most appropriate for the supervisor to exercise. Figure 4-5 provides guidelines that will help you make that decision.

See Section 21 for a complete discussion of the use of varied levels of control depending upon teacher type.

### Figure 4-3

**LEVEL OF TEACHING SKILL**

| Aspects | High Degree | Moderate Degree | Low Degree |
|---|---|---|---|
| Instructional Approaches | diagnoses student needs; varies approaches using the most appropriate for each situation; motivates students using past experiences; varies questions; uses mostly high-level questions | aware of the needs of some students; uses the most convenient approach for each situation; sometimes motivates before presentation; varies questions; uses mostly low-level questions | unaware or unconcerned with student needs; uses one type of approach for all situations; does not motivate before presentation; little variety; uses all low-level questions |
| Materials Selection | uses materials of all modalities; uses materials effectively; seeks new materials | uses materials that are easiest to find; uses materials effectively | uses materials that are on hand; often uses materials ineffectively |
| Management Ability | keeps detailed teacher records; students keep detailed records; class is always under control; frequent use of flexible student grouping | keeps detailed teacher records; students keep some records; when control is lost it is quickly regained; frequent use of static groups | keeps some teacher records; students do not keep records; control is often lost and difficult to regain; grouping is rarely used |

### Figure 4-5

**GUIDELINES FOR LEVEL OF CONTROL DECISIONS**

| Degree of Performance | Teacher Type | Level Of Control |
|---|---|---|
| High in all areas | Master | Total teacher dominance |
| Mostly high/some moderate areas | Outstanding | Teacher dominance |
| Moderate in all areas | Good | Collaboration |
| Mostly moderate/some low areas | Has potential | Supervisor dominance |
| Mostly low | Inexperienced | Total supervisor dominance |

Figure 4-4

## LEVEL OF EFFECTIVENESS ASSESSMENT

| | HIGH DEGREE | MODERATE DEGREE | LOW DEGREE |
|---|---|---|---|
| **Area: Level of Personal Involvement** | | | |
| **Aspects:** | | | |
| **Enthusiasm** | | | |
| **Energy Level** | | | |
| movement | | | |
| involvement | | | |
| seating | | | |
| **Time Commitment** | | | |
| arrival time | | | |
| departure time | | | |
| afternoon meetings | | | |
| evening meetings | | | |
| home contacts | | | |
| **Concern for:** | | | |
| students | | | |
| self-development | | | |
| others | | | |
| school | | | |
| **Area: Ability to Analyze and Solve Problems** | | | |
| **Aspects:** | | | |
| **Identify the Problem** | | | |
| who identifies | | | |
| **Analyze the Situation** | | | |
| examines | | | |
| all sides | | | |
| why and what | | | |
| **Propose Solutions** | | | |
| multiple | | | |
| **Develop a Plan** | | | |
| selection | | | |
| implementation | | | |
| **Area: Level of Teaching Skill** | | | |
| **Aspects:** | | | |
| **Instructional Approaches** | | | |
| diagnoses students | | | |
| varied approaches | | | |
| motivation techniques | | | |
| question variety | | | |
| question level | | | |
| **Materials Selection** | | | |
| varied modalities | | | |
| effective use | | | |
| new materials | | | |
| **Management** | | | |
| teacher records | | | |
| student records | | | |
| class control | | | |
| student grouping | | | |

# How to Diagnose Teacher Needs

# Gathering Data

The improvement of teacher performance begins with a diagnosis of teacher needs, which depends upon effective data-gathering procedures.

## WHAT DATA TO GATHER

There are several characteristics that data should exhibit in order to be effective: it must be related to diagnosis, and it must be objective in nature.

### Related to Diagnosis

Gathered data constitutes important information about the skills and needs of the teacher. The data is most useful when it relates to a particular type of diagnosis, one that examines:

1. The teacher's views and concerns as discussed during a conference
2. The teacher's instruction plans for what, when, how, and with whom

3. What is happening, at a particular point in time, in the teacher's classroom, in the halls outside, and so forth

4. How the teacher's classroom functions as a total learning environment

5. How instructional time is used by the teacher and students

6. What students produce

7. The teacher's performance during delivery of instruction

8. Perceptions of peers and parents about the teacher

## Objective in Nature

Objective data is data that has been observed and can be described. Avoid interpreting the data and making an evaluation for two reasons:

1. Your interpretation may be wrong. *For example, here is a recent classroom episode:* The lesson focused on a discussion of Chapter 3 in *A Tale of Two Cities.* Five students at the back of the room did not participate in the discussion. Rather, they interacted only with each other and did not hear the discussion. *Your observation:* Five students, seated in the back of the room, did not participate in the lesson. *The possible interpretation:* Five students in the back of the room were ignored by the teacher and allowed to miss the lesson. *Teacher's Response:* "Five advanced students had completed the reading of this work in a previous class. They cooperatively agreed upon a critical-thinking project related to the work. They were seated in the back of the room to permit them to begin the brainstorming activity concerned with identifying modern acts of courage."

2. Your interpretation could cause the teacher to become hostile and defensive. *For example, here is a recent classroom episode:* The lesson focused on the initial presentation of division using a two-place divisor. Periodically throughout the lesson, two youngsters spoke and wrote notes to each other. *Your observation:* During this lesson, two youngsters participated, from time to time, in written and oral communication. *The possible interpretation:* Two students were continuously distracted during the lesson. They may not be motivated to learn the topic. *Teacher's Response:* "One of the two youngsters is a recent arrival to this country. The other youngster speaks both English and the foreign language. They were seated together to allow the English-speaking student to help the foreign language student. How do you expect me to teach the curriculum and deal, at the same time, with youngsters who do not speak English? Why are non-English-speaking students always placed in my class?"

# HOW TO GATHER DATA

Gathered data should accurately record the date, time, place, and events observed. This prevents distortion of the facts and a lack of recall when that data is later reviewed as a part of a larger source or specifically in conference with the teacher.

## Printed Form

A printed form sets an all-inclusive standard with which the observed data can be compared. The form may be used in four different ways:

1. To mark what is missing from the standard used
2. To mark what is included, leaving blank what is missing
3. To comment upon various aspects observed or not observed
4. To complete the specifics listed

The printed form is particularly suited to specific types of data gathering, such as:

1. A review of teacher plans
2. An observation of how a classroom functions as a total learning environment
3. An analysis of how instructional time is used by students and teachers
4. Preparation of a pre-observation plan
5. A top sheet for student products

## Notetaking

Other types of data are more easily gathered by taking notes. However, the notetaking will take different forms depending upon what data is gathered.

**Verbatim Notetaking.** This type of notetaking records, as accurately as possible, the exact words and actions of the teacher and the students. It is possible to gather data related to the sequence of the lesson and the interaction between the teacher and the students, as well as the exact questions asked and how they were answered.

Although verbatim notetaking is an excellent tool, it has several limitations:

1. It is often difficult to keep up with the actions and words.
2. Since inflection and tone cannot be recorded, an element of the delivery is lost.
3. It is sometimes difficult to hear a particular response from a student.

Both audio- and videotape are useful in verbatim notetaking. However, each has its limitations and should be used in combination with written notes rather than by itself:

1. Audiotape records only oral data and eliminates other types of visual clues that could be observed. In addition, the tape recorder may not be sensitive enough to pick up the words of those not seated close by. Outside noises may also distort the recording or cause gaps in the material.
2. Videotape can record only one area of the classroom at a time. When the action moves, the focus of the camera may not move quickly enough to catch that action. In addition, some people are not comfortable while being viewed by the camera, which may cause a change in their usual behavior.

Verbatim notetaking is particularly suited to gathering data concerned with the teacher's performance during the delivery of instruction.

**Other Types of Notetaking.**  Some data is best gathered through different forms of notetaking that relate to the specific activity. These include:

1. Summary of a conference
2. Details of statements from peers and parents
3. Comments recorded on top sheets sent with student products
4. Items seen during informal visits


# WHY DATA IS GATHERED

Whenever a supervisor is attempting to assess an individual's performance, data must be gathered accurately and in detail.


## To Diagnose Teacher Skills and Needs

The purpose of conducting a diagnosis is to determine teacher skills and needs so an appropriate supervision plan can be formed. Each of the eight types of diagnoses presented in Figure 5-1 focuses on a different aspect of teacher performance and contributes valuable data for analysis. You may not find it necessary to conduct all eight diagnoses with each teacher, but you will want to have sufficient data to analyze. If you cannot come to a specific conclusion about a supervisory plan, you probably do not have enough data.


## To Determine a Supervision Plan

Once teacher skills and needs are diagnosed, they can be matched to an appropriate supervision plan. Part III deals with how to make this match and presents each supervision plan in detail.


## To Provide Feedback to the Teacher

Following each diagnosis, some form of feedback should be provided to the teacher. The form of this feedback is directly related to the type of diagnosis conducted. Each type of diagnosis presented in Part II will present a suggested form for feedback to teachers.

The feedback form may or may not include an invitation to a conference. An invitation to a conference is required only if:

1. There is a problem that requires immediate correction
2. The supervision plan is ready to be put into action

In other cases, all that is necessary is an acknowledgment of the diagnostic review, which is viewed as a part of the total diagnostic process.

### Figure 5-1

| SPECIFYING THE DIAGNOSTIC TYPES | | | |
|---|---|---|---|
| **Diagnostic Type** | **For Whom** | **When** | **Purpose** |
| Exploration conference | All | Early in the year | Express teacher concern, plans |
| Teacher plans | All | Ongoing | Monitor progress through the curriculum Confirm action plan |
| Informal visits | All | Ongoing | Monitor instruction Confirm plans |
| Classroom environment | All | October through November | Evaluate the total classroom environment |
| Time-on-task review | Disruptive classes Investigate complaints | Ongoing | How instructional time is used by students and teachers |
| Student products | All | Ongoing | View progress |
| Formal exploration visit | New teacher Inexperienced teacher Marginal teacher | Early in the year | Overview of teacher delivery skills |
| Reported data | All | Ongoing | Sensitivity to changes, concerns, and problems |

# Holding Exploration Conferences

The exploration conference is appropriate for every member of your instructional staff. The conferences should be held individually, early in the school year. These conferences are the major supervisory activity for the first month of the school year.

## REASONS FOR CONDUCTING THESE CONFERENCES

The purpose of the exploration conference is to give you the teacher's point of view about everything that interacts with the delivery of instruction.

### Expectations for the Year

The teacher should be encouraged to discuss his or her plans, hopes, and dreams for the year. The discussion may include the application of an in-service course in which the teacher was involved or the implementation of a new curriculum.

The concerns that the teacher has about reaching the dreams that are planned should be expressed. It is important to identify the possible constraints that may prevent the plan from becoming a reality. Some sample supervisory leads are:

1. *"How do you plan to deal with clarifying homework assignments?"*
2. *"How will the in-service course you took in writing change your program?"*
3. *"What problems do you foresee in implementing the newly mandated social studies curriculum?"*

## Subject Matter

A discussion of specific subject matter should be included in the conference. The teacher should identify the way in which the curriculum will be presented to students with different needs. The discussion should cover all the teacher's areas of responsibility.

In the elementary school, the teacher should present a grouping plan for both reading and mathematics, organizing the groups according to the levels of ability of the students in the class. The plan must include all the students for whom the teacher is responsible. Other subjects which are within the teacher's areas of responsibility, such as language arts, science, music, art, and so forth, should also be discussed. The specified plan should include the frequency and time frames for the group meetings. Provision for review and reinforcement, individual differences, and homework should also be discussed.

In the secondary school, the teacher should present a plan for presentation of content that provides for individual differences among classes. The supervisory discussion should cover how to deal with those students who do not appear to grasp a concept after the first teaching. A plan for the use of a variety of instructional methods including lecture, class discussion, group work, and individual projects should be discussed. Plans for review and reinforcement using classwork, homework, and interdisciplinary topics can also be explored. Some sample supervisory leads are:

1. *"How will you address the range of reading ability in your classes?"*
2. *"How will homework assignments be varied for differences in ability?"*
3. *"How will you incorporate writing skills into your social studies program?"*

## Materials

The teacher should specify the materials that will be used with each group or class of students. The materials should be suited to the content and levels of ability of the students.

In addition, the materials should provide for differences in learning style so that students have the opportunity to work with oral, visual, tactile, and kinesthetic materials. The teacher's plans should include finding, making, and requesting the types of materials suited to the content of the subject matter. Problems concerned with a lack of appropriate materials should be stated. Some sample supervisory leads are:

1. *"What reading material will you use with the below-level group?"*
2. *"Which text do you plan to use with the honors class?"*
3. *"What type of manipulative materials will you use to teach those mathematics concepts?"*

## Classroom Management

The way in which the classroom will be organized for instruction should be presented by the teacher. This will include: the seating arrangement, teacher records, student records, procedures for giving and checking homework, and receiving and distributing materials and assignments.

A discussion of classroom management also includes effective use of time. The teacher's plan should include: how and where to gather instructional groups, the use of transition time, and how to deal with routines.

The teacher should discuss the code of behavior that will be established with the class. A plan to achieve good control of the group and to deal with discipline problems should be presented. Some sample supervisory leads are:

1. *"How and when will assigned homework be checked?"*
2. *"What items do you consider important to record?"*
3. *"What steps will you take to control a youngster who is acting out?"*

## Student Population

The teacher should discuss and be informed about the students for whom he or she is responsible. This includes the variety of academic abilities, learning needs, and special problems of the youngsters. Some sample supervisory leads are:

1. *"What is the range of ability among your students?"*
2. *"Are there wide differences in ability among the students in the honors class?"*
3. *"What proportion of the students in your class are non-English-speaking?"*
4. *"Are any of your students learning disabled?"*
5. *"Have you been informed about the death of Harry's mother?"*
6. *"Have you spoken with the outside counseling agency and the guidance counselor about Mary?"*

## Personal Problems

The teacher may wish to use this opportunity to discuss some personal problems. It is to the teacher's benefit to make you aware of any personal situation that may affect attendance, lateness, and effectiveness. These are usually sensitive issues. The teacher may choose to share, or not to share, the issue with you. Trust and sensitivity between you and the teacher may help him or her reveal the problem. Some sample supervisory leads are:

1. *"How is everything at home?"*
2. *"I have noticed that you do not smile very often."*
3. *"You were frequently absent last spring. Is anything wrong?"*

# HOW TO RECORD THE DATA FROM THE CONFERENCE

A record of the exploration conference is kept by writing summary notes. This can be done in two ways:

1. Recording a running summary of what was discussed.
2. Organizing the notes under each item that was discussed.

Organizing your summary will make notetaking easier and your notes of more value when they are reviewed at a later date. A sample form for recording the exploration conference is presented in Figure 6-1.

# HOW TO USE THE DATA FROM THE CONFERENCE

There are at least four ways in which the data from the exploration conference can be used:

1. To provide insight
2. To identify immediate needs
3. As a self-evaluation
4. As an initial diagnosis

## Provide Insight

Data from a well-organized exploration conference gives the supervisor an opportunity to see the total instructional program from the teacher's pont of view. It

**Figure 6-1**

**EXPLORATION CONFERENCE SUMMARY**

**ITEMS/COMMENTS**

**Expectations:** _____
_____
_____
_____
_____

**Subject Matter:** _____
_____
_____
_____

**Materials:** _____
_____
_____
_____
_____

**Classroom Management:** _____
_____
_____
_____
_____

**Student Population:** _____
_____
_____

_____
**Teacher's Signature**

_____
**Supervisor's Signature**

provides an overview of all of the aspects with which the teacher will deal during the year.

During the conference the teacher will reveal important information concerned with skills and needs. This includes:

1. Areas in which change is desired
2. Aspects of instruction that could be improved
3. Areas of insecurity
4. Items that are potential problems
5. How to organize for instruction
6. How to use time efficiently
7. How to provide for individual differences
8. Selection and use of specific materials
9. Relationship of materials to students' needs
10. Dealing with a lack of materials
11. Management of the classroom
12. Maintaining order and discipline
13. Sensitivity to the needs of individual students
14. Understanding the problems of individuals and groups

## Immediate Needs

The needs and problems of the teacher that require immediate attention are revealed through the conference. It is then possible to take steps to correct them as quickly as possible. Immediate needs may include:

1. Students being placed in inappropriate classes
2. Instructional materials that must be ordered
3. Physical needs of the classroom
4. Scheduling changes

## Self-Evaluation

The exploration conference may serve as a self-evaluation for both master and outstanding teachers. It provides these superior teachers with the opportunity to analyze what they have done and to begin planning ways to improve those efforts. It is the first step in their identification of the areas on which they will focus. This initial analysis will later be used in the supervisory plan.

### Initial Diagnosis

The exploration conference provides the supervisor an opportunity to make an initial diagnosis of teacher needs for most of the teachers on staff. It gives valuable insight about what each teacher plans to do and how each teacher functions. At this point, however, the data is incomplete. This initial diagnosis will be confirmed or changed as additional data is received. At that time an effective supervisory plan can be selected.

The supervisor's role at the exploration conference is as data gatherer. Suggestions should be minimal. However, there are two instances when suggestions should be given:

1. Items that must be changed. For example, the teacher proposes to work with five reading groups. You may wish to suggest other ways to organize the reading groups so no more than three will be necessary. Or, the teacher has selected a material that is inappropriate for a particular group and you suggest an alternative.

2. Minor points of improvement. For example, advising an inexperienced teacher to assign an English-speaking buddy to each non-English-speaking student, preferably one who speaks the same foreign language. Or suggesting a source for free materials related to the teacher's topic of interest.

## PROVIDING FEEDBACK TO THE TEACHER

You should record notes during the conference. These notes will include all the items discussed, the teacher's comments, and any suggestions that you have made.

At the conclusion of the conference, ask the teacher to read the notes and sign them. Then give the teacher a copy of the notes.

Following the conference, review the notes. You might find it helpful to record, on a separate sheet of paper, additional comments about the conference or make special reference to a comment on your original notes. This will help you form an initial diagnosis of teacher skills and needs.

# Reviewing Teacher Plans

Continually reviewing the teacher plans of every member of the instructional staff is a powerful and appropriate diagnostic tool for the supervisor.

## WHY SHOULD YOU LOOK AT PLANS?

There are at least two purposes to be accomplished by reviewing teacher plans: (1) to determine the teacher's attitudes, and (2) to clarify instructional plans.

### To Determine Teacher Attitudes

Determining teacher attitudes involves four aspects, as described here:

**Comprehensiveness.** The plans should include all the areas for which the teacher is responsible.

**Organization.** The plans should be written in an easily understood manner. They should be neat and appropriate for the teacher's reference.

**Detail.** There should be sufficient detail about the

content of the material to clarify what, how, and when each is intended to be presented in the instructional program.

**Creativity.** There should be indicators of variety in the instructional presentation and materials planned to motivate and excite student interest.

### To Clarify Instructional Plans

Clarifying instructional plans involves the following seven points. It is done to ensure that instruction is carried out in an appropriate manner.

**Monitor Movement Through the Curriculum.** The planned instruction should reflect progress at an appropriate pace through the established curriculum.

**Coverage of All Aspects.** Plans should include all aspects of each curriculum for which the teacher is responsible without inappropriate weight on any one aspect.

**Differentiation.** The plans should specify how provision will be made for students with different abilities and needs.

**Variety of Instructional Techniques.** Plans should indicate variety in instructional presentation, including lecture, teacher demonstration, student discussion, small group interaction, student-to-student interaction, and individual tasks.

**Variety of Materials Used.** Plans should indicate variety in instructional materials used to reach objectives. This variety includes texts, reference materials, periodicals, newspapers, worksheets, audio and visual media, and manipulatives.

**Monitor Progress on the Selected Supervisory Plan.** Areas of concentration decided upon for the supervisory plan should be included in the teacher's plans, such as a listing of the specific questions that will be asked, stated motivations for various lessons, or specific grouping practices.

**Comparison.** The plans of teachers of the same grade or subject may be compared to determine pace and subject coverage.

## WHEN AND HOW SHOULD YOU COLLECT PLANS?

Plans should be reviewed periodically throughout the year. Some of the problems that occur when collecting and reviewing plans can be avoided by following these rules:

**1. Never collect plans you will not read and comment on.** If teacher plans are not important enough to be read, why should teachers spend time writing them? Teachers know if their plans are read. You may find notes to you in the plans, or a teacher may ask you what you thought of a particular technique that he or she had written. It is also possible that a teacher whose plans were poorly written, in great haste, will be left with the impression that what was done is perfectly acceptable.

2. **Never keep teacher plans more than one day.** Teachers use their plans to implement instruction. If this is not true, then there is little reason for teachers to plan! If you are slow in returning teacher plans, how can teachers use them?

## Collecting Teacher Plans

It is very important to collect and review teacher plans, but the method and manner can vary with your situation. Several methods are described here.

**Plans of All Teachers Are Collected Every Week.** This strategy may be very desirable but not too practical, especially if you have a large staff. A great deal of time will be taken up with reviewing all these plans and little else will be accomplished.

**Rotation.** The plans of different groups of teachers are collected every two or three weeks. Each teacher's plans for the two- or three-week interval are then reviewed. There are two advantages to this strategy: (1) each week you review a smaller number of plans, and (2) you are able to see a two- or three-week sequence of activities.

Teacher plans may be grouped for rotation by whatever system you find most convenient, such as grade level, subject area(s), department(s), or location in the building.

**Differentiation.** You may find it desirable to further provide for teacher needs by collecting the plans of inexperienced or weak teachers each week and collecting the plans of master and outstanding teachers once a month.

Be sure to communicate the collection strategy you have decided upon to the staff. They should be informed about both when and how their plans will be reviewed.

# HOW TO RECORD DATA WHEN REVIEWING PLANS

A printed memo is both an easy and an effective way in which to record data gathered when reviewing teacher plans because:

1. The memo serves as a comprehensive list of what should be included in the plans.
2. Areas and specifics omitted from the plans can be checked.
3. A copy of the annotated printed memo can be kept.
4. The annotated original can be sent to the teacher when the plans are returned.

The sample printed memos are intended to be a suggested list of what should be included in teacher plans. You may wish to modify the list to fit the specifics of your school program. Figure 7-1 suggests a printed plan memo for elementary schools. Figure 7-2 suggests a printed plan memo for secondary schools.

## HOW TO USE THE DATA AFTER YOUR REVIEW

You should keep a copy of your notations on the printed plan memo. If you have checked areas or specifics omitted or questioned, the teacher is expected to respond. It is helpful to add the teacher's response to your copy of the plan memo. Or, if the teacher returns the original with comments, substitute the original for your copy.

The plan review memos should be kept sequentially for each teacher. They will serve three useful purposes:

1. You can refer back to former comments when you review future plans.
2. You will be able to establish a pattern of weaknesses in both planning and instruction, such as, extensive use of texts, lack of variety in instructional presentation, or frequently omitted content areas.
3. Through informal visits to the classroom, you will be able to verify that what is planned is what is actually being done.

## PROVIDING FEEDBACK TO THE TEACHER

You should initial, date, and write a comment, if appropriate, directly on the teacher's plans. Only commendable comments should be written directly on the plans; other types of comments should be recorded on the printed plan memo. There are few things more demoralizing for a teacher than to see negative comments written on his or her lesson plans by the supervisor.

Just as negative comments are demoralizing, positive comments written on teacher's plans are encouraging. Comment on a plan for a creative idea, implementation of a suggestion made during a conference, or movement as agreed upon in the supervisory plan. For example, write comments such as:

1. *"I look forward to seeing the results of your plan to develop writing skills using a science content."*
2. *"Your plan for brainstorming causes and consequences of the Civil War should have good results."*
3. *"You selected excellent manipulative materials to teach subtraction with exchange."*
4. *"Please keep me informed about your exciting plans to team teach the unit with Ms. Foster."*

The annotated plan memo is used only for teacher plan correction and/or improvement. When a teacher receives a plan review memo, the teacher must initial and return the memo with:

1. Revised, corrected, improved plans,
2. An explanation, or
3. A request for a conference with the supervisor.

## Figure 7-1

**ELEMENTARY**          **PLAN REVIEW MEMO**

To: _____ (initial & return) _____

From: _____

Re: Your plans dated _____

**TOTAL AREAS OF RESPONSIBILITY (items checked are omitted on your plans)**

_____ reading instruction (all groups)_____frequency of instruction

_____ mathematics instruction (all groups)_____frequency of instruction

_____ social studies (unit title)

_____ communication arts (written/oral)

_____ science

_____ art

_____ music

_____ physical education

_____ homework (all areas)

_____ library skills

_____ computer education

_____ progress reports for students in pull-out programs

**SPECIFICS (items checked are omitted on your plans)***

_____ lesson objective(s) (see #    written on your plans)

_____ instructional materials (see #    written on your plans)

_____ pages covered (see #    written on your plans)

_____ class or group lesson (see #    written on your plans)

**COMMENTS**

_____ plans are late

_____ plans are not clear

_____ plans are insufficient

_____ please see me _____

_____ other _____

_____

*For your reference, a number has been written on your plans related to the item(s) checked.

Figure 7-2

**SECONDARY**                    **PLAN REVIEW MEMO**

**To:** _____ (initial & return) _____
**From:** _____
**Re: Your plans dated** _____

**TOTAL AREAS OF RESPONSIBILITY (items checked are omitted on your plans)**

____ all subjects taught          subjects missing _____

____ all grade levels             grade levels missing _____

____ all ability levels           ability level(s) missing _____

____ homework assigned            class missing _____

____ administrative responsibilities

____ progress reports for students in pull-out programs

**SPECIFICS (items checked are omitted on your plans)***

____ unit topic (see #    written on your plans)

____ lesson objective(s) (see #    written on your plans)

____ presentation type (see #    written on your plans)

____ instructional materials (see #    written on your plans)

____ pages to be covered (see #    written on your plans)

____ class or group lesson (see #    written on your plans)

____ stated ongoing project(s) (see #    written on your plans)

**COMMENTS**

____ plans are late

____ plans are not clear

____ plans are insufficient

____ please see me _____

____ other _____

_____

*For your reference, a number has been written on your plans related to the item(s) checked.

# Making Informal Visits

Valuable data can be gathered when making informal visits. All areas of the school are appropriate places for these visits. This includes classrooms, special program rooms, cafeteria, auditorium, gymnasium, library, computer rooms, and all other areas used by the school population.

## REASONS FOR MAKING INFORMAL VISITS

Informal visits can help you accomplish a variety of objectives, such as:

### To Determine What Is Actually Happening

You are provided with a firsthand view of what is actually going on—a candid picture of the room, teacher, and students, at that point in time for your review and assessment. This view is, of course, representative but is probably very close to the usual since it is unplanned.

## To Confirm Teacher Plans

The informal visits make it possible to confirm that what the teacher has written in his or her plans is what is really being done in the classroom. For example, you may be concerned with the rate of progress of the reading groups in a particular class. The informal visit will enable you to note what lesson each reading group is working on. Compare those lesson numbers with the ones stated in that teacher's plans.

## To Monitor Progress

You will be able to determine if certain suggestions you made to the teacher are being implemented. For example, you may have discussed a plan to improve the use of the chalkboard. You can see how well those suggestions have been used by glancing at the board. It is also possible to monitor progress with certain aspects of the supervisory action plan. For example, part of the supervisory plan may be concerned with improvement of teacher questions. During the informal visit, make it a point to listen to several of the questions that the teacher is asking at that moment. You will know immediately if the teacher is improving and if that effort to improve is a part of the teacher's daily actions or those reserved only for formal observations. Student actions may also be monitored during the informal visit. You may want to talk to a newly admitted child or just observe the way in which the child appears to interact with other classmates. You may wish to check the behavior of a particular youngster who has been having problems.

## To Look for Potential Trouble Spots

The visits may make it possible to spot a potential problem. By spotting and intercepting a note passed between two youngsters you may prevent a planned fight. After watching a youngster having difficulty with an exchange problem, you may note that no representative materials are available for that student's use. As you walk around the room you may spot some previously unnoticed loose floor tiles.

## To Make Yourself Visible

The supervisor's appearance in and around the school makes everyone believe that you care, that you are interested in and involved with the teachers and the students. Both students and teachers may use the opportunity of your informal visits to show you something they are very proud of. Or, they may stop you to ask a question or make a complaint about something of which you were not aware. You can respond immediately with praise or an assurance that you will investigate the complaint and get back to them if necessary.

# THE IMPORTANCE OF A TIME FRAME FOR MAKING INFORMAL VISITS

The objectives of the informal visits are better met if the visits are unannounced and ongoing throughout the year. This does not mean, however, that your visits are unplanned.

The informal visit is most effective if you develop a system or plan for its use. The plan that you select must fit your needs and schedule.

## How Often to Visit

Every classroom should be visited every day. This may not be possible if you have a large school. Certain busy times of the year may also make this practice periodically impossible. Visiting two to three times a week is a good alternative to the daily visit. At the very least, classrooms should be visited once a week.

## Whom to Visit

If visits cannot be made on a daily basis, it is wise to plan whom to visit each day so that you do get around to everyone. The visit plan is a matter of personal preference. Here are some suggested groupings for your visits:

| | |
|---|---|
| one grade | all grade 7 or grade 1 classes |
| one department | all English or social studies classes |
| ability level | all honors classes or classes for gifted |
| ability levels | honors classes and remediation classes; gifted classes and below-grade-level classes |
| building plan | all top floor classes; all lower level classes; all east wing classes |
| all special programs | English second language, learning disability, remediation, computer education classes |

## Time of Day for Visits

Informal visits are most effective when the time of day is varied. Visits should be scheduled to take place during prime instructional time as well as during the time of day, such as late morning or afternoon, that is most difficult in the classroom.

## How Long to Stay

The informal visit is intended to be brief. You will find that between two and ten minutes is adequate. How long you stay will depend on what you see and what you are looking for.

# RECORDING THE DATA FROM AN INFORMAL VISIT

Notetaking is the most effective way to record data gathered from informal visits. The rules that follow are helpful hints:

1. Always carry a pencil and paper when making informal visits. If possible, keep the pad out of sight. If this is not possible, you may well become known as the supervisor with the clipboard.

2. Avoid taking notes while you are in the classroom. This activity seems to make teachers nervous. Instead, record mentally what, if anything, appears to be significant. There will be times when all you will wish to note is that you made the informal visit. An exception to this rule is whenever a teacher or student stops you to ask a question or make a request. Be sure that person sees you write down what was asked or requested.

3. Record your mental notes as soon as possible after leaving the classroom. Usually that is best done in the hall. If you wait until you return to the office, you may forget important pieces or parts of what you saw. This is especially true when you are making several informal visits in a row.

4. Have a mental outline of what to look for. This includes:

| | |
|---|---|
| teacher attitude | voice, body language, facial expression, actions, gestures |
| teacher activity | what the teacher is doing, whether instructing the class, a group or an individual; conducting a lecture, discussion, or demonstration; observing, assisting, or correcting |
| teacher location | seated or standing, apart from the students, at the teacher's desk, at a student's desk, in front of the class, sitting with a group |

| materials in use | variety and type, whether textbooks, worksheets, media, supplementary books, or no materials in use and desks clear |
| --- | --- |
| student activity | what the students are doing; whether working with the teacher, with a group or a peer, working independently, or off-task |
| room management | how the students use the room, the noise level, behavior of the students, established code or rules |
| room appearance | neatness, organization, placement of materials, students' seating pattern, temperature and light, general attractiveness |
| specific concerns | areas of interest to the supervisor, such as confirming teacher plans, monitoring progress, checking implementation of suggestions, spotting potential trouble, checking student progress |

5. Do not disrupt the instructional program. Use body language rather than speech. Smile and nod as you enter and leave. Be sure you are seen by the teacher. Speak only if spoken to or if you have something important to say, and avoid getting into a discussion with the teacher. If you must speak to the teacher, ask him or her to see your privately.

## HOW TO USE THE DATA

Record your mental notes as soon as you have left the classroom. Later, when you return to the office, transfer those notes to a more permanent place. Be sure to record the date and the time of the informal visit. These notes become a part of the total data gathered and are used to help you make a decision about which supervisory plan is most effective for that teacher. After the supervisory plan has been selected and implemented, the notes will help you to:

1. Monitor the teacher's progress on the supervisory plan
2. Check the teacher's skill development in particular areas
3. Determine if more work is needed on a particular skill
4. Identify new skill needs

## PROVIDING FEEDBACK TO THE TEACHER

Every informal visit does not require that feedback be provided to the teacher. This is especially true if:

1. Informal visits are a part of your daily schedule for all classrooms.

2. Informal visits are not new or different from what has been done in the past.

3. The staff expects and accepts your informal visits.

4. Nothing unusual or exceptional was seen.

Informal visits require feedback to teachers if:

1. The visits are infrequent.

2. They are a new action.

3. Teachers are anxious about the visits.

4. Something unusual or exceptional was seen.

5. You wish to make a suggestion related to what you saw.

Feedback to teachers about informal visits to their classrooms should:

1. Be objective in nature

2. Usually communicate a commendable item

3. Offer minor suggestions

Items of serious nature or ones that require extensive skill development should become a part of the supervisory action plan. The informal visit may speed up the selection and implementation of a specific supervisory action plan.

When a teacher does receive feedback from you about an informal visit, be sure to keep a copy of the memo. (See Figure 8-1.)

The following are some sample supervisory comments for feedback to teachers:

### Commendation of effective teacher actions

1. *"You used excellent critical-thinking questions during the class discussion of the outcomes of the Revolutionary War."*

2. *"This morning, your students demonstrated that their skills in analyzing and then solving problems are well-developed."*

3. *"Your use of small peer groups to improve students' writing efforts is both outstanding and commendable."*

### Suggestions for improvement

1. *"Mary appears to be having difficulty with exchange. Please order squared materials to help her."*

2. *"This afternoon I noticed several loose floor tiles in the back of your classroom. Have you reported this?"*

3. *"Please speak to the librarian. Several new reference books, dealing with the topic under study in your social studies classes, are now available."*

### Comments not appropriate for feedback to teachers

1. *"Your questioning techniques need improvement. You ask mainly 'yes' or 'no' questions."*

2. *"Your management of the classroom is ineffective. You should better organize your room, establish a code of behavior, and try a behavior modification program."*

**Figure 8-1**

**MEMO**

**To:**
**From:**
**Re: Informal Visit**
**Date** _____ **Time** _____

**Comment**

_____

_____

# Observing Classroom Environments

The structure, activity, and organization of the classroom dramatically affect learning. Yet, these essential elements of instruction are rarely the focus of an observation. That is why it is important to observe all classroom environments early in the school year.

## PURPOSE OF OBSERVING CLASSROOM ENVIRONMENTS

Observe the classroom to determine the overall effectiveness of the learning environment. To accomplish this, focus on three important aspects of the classroom: (1) the roles of the teacher, (2) the activities of the students, and (3) the organization for encouraging student involvement.

### Roles of the Teacher

The teacher performs three important roles in the classroom, each of which contributes to the effective and efficient performance of the classroom as a maximum learning environment. The roles are:

1. **Diagnostician of needs**—The teacher identifies the individual's and group's skill and modality needs.
3. **Instructor**—The teacher provides for instruction of skills in areas of needs using materials and techniques appropriate for each student.
3. **Manager**—The teacher organizes the total learning environment so that it helps students work effectively, comfortably, and purposefully.

A full discussion of these three roles is shown in Figure 9-1. Each role has been matched to the visible aspects of the role that can be observed.

## Activities of the Students

The students are involved in three areas of participation in the classroom. Each area of participation contributes to the student's success as a learner. The observable behaviors show students:

1. **Involved in on-task activities**—The students work with various groupings, the class, a peer, or independently, to accomplish learning tasks.
2. **Using materials**—The students use materials of different modalities, levels, and skill needs as each requires. These materials are used appropriately and productively.
3. **Managing their own instruction**—Students are responsible for completing their work and conducting themselves in an appropriate manner.

A full discussion of these areas is given in Figure 9-2. Each area has been matched to the visible aspects of the area that can be observed.

## Organization for Encouraging Student Involvement

There are two areas of classroom organization that encourage student involvement. Each is essential to providing an environment that offers the maximum opportunity for student learning. They are:

1. **Materials**—Materials are readily available and are appropriate to the students' skill needs and modalities.
2. **Appearance**—The appearance of the room is an incentive to learning.

A full discussion of these two areas is given in Figure 9-3. Each area has been matched to the visible aspects that can be observed.

Figure 9-1

## A TEACHER'S THREE ROLES

### Teacher Role 1: Diagnostician of Needs

| In the performance of this role, the teacher: | The visible aspects of this role include: |
| --- | --- |
| tests student mastery of concepts | students' tests on display, kept in folders or in notebooks |
| questions students' in-depth understanding | teacher asking questions of individuals or groups of students |
| checks students' classwork and homework | classwork and homework in student notebooks have the teacher's initials, check, star, etc. |
| corrects students' classwork and homework | classwork and homework in student notebooks have the teacher's notations, comments, suggestions, etc. |
| observes students working in the classroom | the teacher walking around the room, looking at students' work, talking to students |
| groups students for instruction by skill need(s) | student groups listed on the board, on charts, in record books |
| moves about the room to be involved with students | the teacher walking around the room, sitting with groups and individuals |

### Teacher Role 2: Instructor

| In the performance of this role, the teacher: | The visible aspects of this role include: |
| --- | --- |
| instructs the whole class | results of tests or informal diagnoses indicate all students need instruction in this skill |
| instructs groups of students | results of tests or informal diagnoses indicate students in the group need instruction in this skill |
| instructs individuals | results of tests or informal diagnosis indicate individual student needs instruction in this skill |

### Teacher Role 3: Manager of the Learning Environment

| In the performance of this role, the teacher: | The visible aspects of this role include: |
| --- | --- |
| plans instruction for the class and for individuals | plans recorded in the teacher's written plans, in record books, on the chalkboard |
| controls the behavior of the students in the classroom | students speaking softly when allowed, sitting in appropriate areas, conducting themselves appropriately |
| keeps students on-task | students occupied in appropriate and meaningful work |
| keeps records of student achievement and progress | teacher's record book containing grades, assessments, comments |

Figure 9-2

## ACTIVITIES OF STUDENTS

### Student Area 1: Involved in On-Task Activities

When involved in on-task activities, students work:

| | |
|---|---|
| as members of a class group | all of the students involved and attentive during a class lesson |
| as members of a group | groups of students involved and attentive during a group lesson |
| in peer groups | groups of two or three students working together |
| independently on assigned tasks | individual students involved and attentive to particular tasks |

The visible aspects of this area include:

### Student Area 2: Using Materials

In completing tasks, students use materials:

The visible aspects of this area include:

| | |
|---|---|
| of varied modalities (oral, visual, tactile, kinesthetic) appropriate to their learning styles | students working with print, tapes, films, and manipulatives by self-selection or assignment |
| on different levels appropriate to their ability levels | students working with materials on different levels (on, below, above grade) as appropriate |
| in different parts of the classroom | students working in all parts of the classroom |
| in productive ways | students producing products |
| with respect and care | students using materials carefully, appropriately, without abuse |

### Student Area 3: Managing Their Own Instruction

Students demonstrate responsibility for their instruction by:

The visible aspects of this area include:

| | |
|---|---|
| keeping records of their work and progress | students keeping samples of their work, test scores, comments made by the teacher on their work |
| planning the activities with which they are involved | students planning how, when, where, with what, and with whom they will complete projects |
| checking the work completed by themselves and peers | students checking their work and the work of classmates |
| giving and receiving assistance when necessary | students helping each other, giving suggestions, assistance, and clarification |
| showing respect for others in the classroom | students listening to each other, talking, smiling |
| using the established rules of the classroom | students following an established pattern for leaving their seats, leaving the room, talking, working, etc. |
| following a code of behavior expected of them | students speaking softly, politely, and acting in appropriate ways |
| moving freely but purposefully and quietly | students walking freely about the room to select, use, and return materials and work |

**Figure 9-3**

### CLASSROOM ORGANIZATION

**Classroom Organization Area 1: Materials**

| The organization of the classroom demonstrates materials are: | The visible aspects of materials organization include: |
|---|---|
| visible in the classroom | visible appearance of materials |
| varied to provide for all learning styles | materials that are oral, visual, tactile, kinesthetic (print, film, manipulatives) |
| neatly arranged | similar materials grouped together, piled, arranged, stacked |
| easily available for student use | placement of materials on levels and in areas that students can reach |

**Classroom Organization Area 2: Appearance**

| The appearance of the classroom's organization demonstrates: | The visible aspects of the classroom's appearance include: |
|---|---|
| furniture arranged to suit instruction | student chairs and desks are grouped for class, group, and individual work |
| instructional areas available | space set aside for teacher/student groups, student groups, individuals |
| student work on display | bulletin boards filled with current student products |
| cleanliness | teacher and student desks are free of excess paper, floors free of paper and dust |
| an attractive setting | an appealing and cheerful total arrangement of the furniture, materials, and display |
| adequate lighting | all light bulbs are working, shades are open or drawn to suit need |
| comfortable temperature | windows are open or shut, students closer or farther away from the heat as desired |

## HOW TO RECORD THE DATA AFTER YOUR CLASSROOM OBSERVATION

Data about the classroom environment is easily recorded using a printed form. (See Figure 9-4.) This form contains all the items discussed as contributing to an effective and efficient classroom learning environment. Some of the items may be observed in action, such as the teacher walking about the room or students working in groups. Other items, such as teacher comments on students' work, materials and furniture arrangements, and bulletin board displays, can be observed as the result of past actions. It is advisable to become familiar with the printed form before using it in a classroom environment so that you know what to look for.

When using the form, keep these points in mind:

1. Check the items observed (both current and past actions).
2. Qualify the teacher roles and organization areas by using this code:
   5 = outstanding, 4 = excellent, 3 = good, 2 = fair, 1 = poor.
3. Qualify student areas by using this code: A = all of the students, M = most of the students, S = some of the students, N = none of the students.
4. Account for items lacking by leaving the spaces blank.
5. Record specific observations next to each item, if necessary.
6. Make additional comments in the lower right corner, if necessary.

## HOW TO USE THE DATA FROM YOUR OBSERVATION

The data gathered from the "Classroom Environment Observation Form" contains valuable information about classroom structure, activity, and organization. The information contributes to a growing body of knowledge that helps you specify the skills and weaknesses of each teacher.

Both you and the teacher should sign and keep a copy of the observation form. Your copy will help you to:

1. Refer back to comments and impressions
2. Group teacher needs
3. Relate environment shortcomings to other areas of teacher weaknesses
4. Develop a supervisory action plan

## PROVIDING FEEDBACK TO THE TEACHER

The results of your classroom environment observation should be reviewed with the teacher during a conference. It is important for the teacher to understand the overall effectiveness of his or her classroom.

This conference should focus on items that are easily corrected, such as techniques for classwork and homework checking, techniques for classwork and homework correction, strategies for keeping records, selection of materials, organization of

Figure 9-4

## CLASSROOM ENVIRONMENT OBSERVATION FORM

Scale: 5 = outstanding  4 = excellent  
3 = good  2 = fair  1 = poor

Scale: A = all  M = most  
S = some  N = none

### TEACHER ROLES

**Diagnostician of Needs**  
Observations

ACTIVITIES  
_____ tests  
_____ questions  
_____ checks classwork  
_____ checks homework  
_____ corrects classwork  
_____ observes  
_____ groups for instruction  
_____ moves about

**Instructor**  
Observations

_____ instructs whole class  
_____ instructs groups  
_____ instructs individuals  
_____ plans instruction  
_____ controls behavior  
_____ keeps students on-task  
_____ keeps progress records

**Manager of the Environment**  
Observations

### ORGANIZATION OF THE CLASSROOM

**Materials**  
Observations

ACTIVITIES  
_____ visible  
_____ varied for learning style  
_____ different levels of ability  
_____ neatly arranged  
_____ easily available  
_____ furniture arranged to suit  
_____ instructional areas  
_____ students' work displayed

**Appearance**  
Observations

_____ clean  
_____ attractive  
_____ adequate lighting  
_____ comfortable temperature

### STUDENT AREAS

**On-Task Activities**  
Observations

ACTIVITIES  
_____ class group  
_____ group  
_____ peer group  
_____ independently

**Using Materials**  
Observations

_____ varied modalities  
_____ different levels  
_____ productively  
_____ with respect/care

**Managing Own Instruction**  
Observations

_____ keep records  
_____ plan activities  
_____ check work  
_____ give/get help  
_____ respect others  
_____ use rules  
_____ follow code of behavior  
_____ move freely  
_____ move quietly

Teacher _____  Class _____  Date _____

Comments:

Teacher's Signature _____  Supervisor's Signature

materials, furniture arrangement, neatness and cleanliness of the classroom, room displays, and student care and use of materials.

Other items that require more extensive supervisory help should be noted and incorporated into the action plan. These may include teacher diagnosis of student skill needs, grouping for instruction, behavior management, keeping students on-task, and managing the classroom.

# Conducting a Time-on-Task Review

The time-on-task review is of great importance because it enables you to focus on each student. School is, of course, a place in which to learn. But students learn only when they are involved and participating. Here is an opportunity to evaluate, within a short time frame, what each individual student within that class is doing.

## WHY SHOULD YOU CONDUCT A TIME-ON-TASK REVIEW?

The purpose of the time-on-task review is to observe each student in the classroom over a fifteen- to thirty-minute time frame to determine the number of students on-task (involved in appropriate activities) and the number of students off-task (involved in non-academic-related activities). In addition, you will be able to analyze the specific types of tasks with which the youngsters are involved. Similarly, you will be able to specify what types of off-task activities are occurring.

## When to Conduct This Review

The time-on-task review is most effective when classroom routines have been established and implemented. The review is intended to assess a fully functioning learning environment. It is therefore better to delay conducting the review until late October.

Every class could benefit from the type of analysis that the time-on-task review offers. When time does not permit you to conduct a review of every class, it is important to conduct the review in the following situations:

1. In classes that are disruptive. Such classes may be noisy as you pass the room. Students may often be out of their seats or may make frequent use of the bathrooms.

2. In classes where large percentages of the students receive poor test scores over a period of time.

3. In classes that have undergone some problem or change. For example, the teacher has been absent a long time or several new students have been admitted within a short period of time.

4. In classes where the teacher appears anxious, depressed, exhausted, or distressed.

5. When there has been a complaint, from a responsible source, that must be checked.

## A Word of Caution

Classrooms reflect the personality of the teacher and are usually different from each other in organization and management. Each time-on-task review should be individual, without comparison to others.

Before you begin to record data, become familiar with the flow and tempo of the classroom. For example, classrooms that are individualized usually have much greater student movement within the room than classrooms that are traditional.

Be aware of distracting factors that may contribute to students' off-task activity. These factors may include a coming school holiday, construction work, or an accident. You may decide that these factors are upsetting enough to prevent your being able to conduct a good review. In this case, postpone the review until another time.

Remember that this telescoped analysis of student actions covers one very short period of time during one day of the school year. The actions observed during the time-on-task review may be representative of what usually happens in that class. On the other hand, you may have observed an unusual day. You will have to make that decision over time.

Classrooms are dynamic settings filled with many people from different homes and backgrounds. It is therefore not at all unusual that they change over time. A time-on-task review may show very different results at different times of the year.

## HOW TO RECORD THE DATA
## FROM A TIME-ON-TASK REVIEW

The time-on-task review data is best recorded using a printed form. (See Figure 10-1.) The form contains a list of areas of student participation. These areas represent student actions that are on-task and those that are off-task. The list of areas of participation may be modified to suit particular class situations.

### On-Task Areas of Participation

On the form, the on-task areas are coded with a single asterisk, and include student actions that are:

1. **Teacher-directed**—All students who are involved with the teacher in any type of activity. This may include whole-class lessons, group lessons, individual student instruction, or discussion.
2. **Group assignment**—All students working in groups of any size without the teacher.
3. **Individual assignment**—All students working by themselves.
4. **Recordkeeping**—All students involved in notation of any kind related to their work. This may include students correcting their work, copying a homework assignment, recording test scores, handing in completed work, and so forth.

### Off-Task Areas of Participation

On the form, the off-task areas are coded with a double asterisk and include student actions identified as:

1. **Transition**—All students between activities. This may include students coming from or going to a group lesson, looking for a book, selecting a task card, looking for a page of notes, returning materials, sharpening a pencil, turning pages, and so forth.
2. **Discipline**—All students involved in disruptive behavior to any degree. This may include fighting, pushing, yelling, acting out, and so forth.

Figure 10-1

# TIME-ON-TASK REVIEW

Class ———— Teacher ———— Date ———— Attendance ————

Time Began ————

| Time Segment | 1 | 2 | 3 | 4 | 5 | 6 | 7 | 8 | 9 | 10 | 11 | 12 | 13 | 14 | 15 | Total |
|---|---|---|---|---|---|---|---|---|---|---|---|---|---|---|---|---|
| *teacher-directed | | | | | | | | | | | | | | | | |
| *group assignment | | | | | | | | | | | | | | | | |
| *individual assignment | | | | | | | | | | | | | | | | |
| *recordkeeping | | | | | | | | | | | | | | | | |
| **transition | | | | | | | | | | | | | | | | |
| **discipline | | | | | | | | | | | | | | | | |
| **unoccupied | | | | | | | | | | | | | | | | |
| **out of room | | | | | | | | | | | | | | | | |
| Total On-Task | | | | | | | | | | | | | | | | |
| Total Off-Task | | | | | | | | | | | | | | | | |
| Total Attending | | | | | | | | | | | | | | | | |

Engagement Rate: $\dfrac{\text{Total On-Task}}{\text{Total Attending}}$ ———— = ———— % On-Task

Comments:

———————————
Teacher's Signature

———————————
Supervisor's Signature

3. **Unoccupied**—All students off assignment. This may include students who are doing nothing, looking out the window, looking around the room, playing with a toy, game, or cards, and so forth.

4. **Out of room**—All students who are not in the classroom for any reason.

You will rapidly become familiar with the listings and their relationship to student actions observed in the classroom. You determine in which area to place each student's actions. Use your own judgment to determine if a particular student action is on- or off-task, but be consistent in that judgment.

## Recording Student Actions

Every student in attendance that day must be accounted for, in a particular area of participation, for each time segment. This means that if thirty students are attending school on that day, there must be a total of thirty accounted for in each time segment.

As previously discussed, the areas of participation represent student actions that are on-task and those that are off-task. Therefore, all the on-task actions plus all the off-task actions must also agree with the total number of students in attendance that day for each time segment.

Figure 10-2 shows a sample recording of student actions for one time segment for a class with thirty students attending.

Figure 10-2

| SAMPLE TIME SEGMENT | | |
| --- | --- | --- |
| **Time Segment** | **1** | **2** |
| *teacher-directed | 10 | |
| *group assignment | 6 | |
| *individual assignment | 8 | |
| *recordkeeping | 2 | |
| **transition | 2 | |
| **discipline | | |
| **unoccupied | 1 | |
| **out of room | 1 | |
| **Total On-Task** | 26 | |
| **Total Off-Task** | 4 | |
| **Total Attending** | 30 | |

During the first time segment of the time-on-task review, each student's action was observed, assigned to an area of participation, and recorded in the appropriate box.

| | |
|---|---|
| teacher-directed | — ten students sat with the teacher in a reading circle. |
| group assignment | — six students were planning to put their individual current events reports into a newscast format for presentation to the class. |
| individual assignment | — eight students worked separately on various tasks. |
| recordkeeping | — one student copied a homework assignment from the board, and one student placed some completed work on the teacher's desk. |
| transition | — one student returned a reference book to the bookcase, and one student turned pages in the math book looking for the assigned page. |
| unoccupied | — one student drank water from the fountain. |
| out of room | — one student was missing and counted as out of the room. |
| Total On-Task | — twenty-six students were involved in on-task areas of participation |
| Total Off-Task | — four students were involved in off-task areas of participation |
| Total Attending | — thirty students were in attendance on that day, so thirty students were accounted for in the first time segment |

## Time Segments

There are a total of fifteen time segments to complete during the time-on-task review. Each time segment should take between one and two minutes to complete. The difference in time is dependent upon the amount of activity and action in the classroom. After you have completed the first time segment you will have a good idea of how much time is needed. Then, use that time frame consistently.

The time segments are recorded sequentially using the time frame that you have set. When there is a great deal of activity in the classroom and you must watch a number of students individually, it may be helpful to use tally marks to record each student's actions correctly. The tally marks in each box can be counted and recorded as a numeral later.

# HOW TO USE THE DATA
# FROM A TIME-ON-TASK REVIEW

There is a large amount of diagnostic information to be gathered from the time-on-task review. This information contributes to the growing fund of knowledge available to guide you in the selection of a supervisory action plan that will help each teacher improve.

Your first task following the time-on-task review is to analyze the data. There are four categories to consider in this analysis:

1. Engagement rate
2. Types of off-task actions noted
3. Types and quality of on-task actions noted
4. Number of students involved in each participation area

## Engagement Rate

The first category to consider is the engagement rate, that is, the percentage of students considered on-task during the time you conducted the review.

To calculate the engagement rate, first add together the total number of students you marked as on-task during each time segment. Record that total in the last column of your score sheet. Then multiply the number of students in attendance that day by fifteen, the total number of observations that you made. Enter that attendance total in the last column of your score sheet. To find the percentage of students on-task, divide the total number of students on-task by the total number attending that day. Here is a sample engagement rate calculation:

$$\frac{\text{Total on-task for the fifteen time segments}}{\text{Total number of students attending } (30 \times 15)} = \frac{375}{450} = 83\%$$

Eighty-three percent of the students in that class were on-task during the time you conducted the time-on-task review. Approximately five students were off-task during each time segment. In order to aim at a higher percentage of on-task activity, analyze what types of off-task actions were noted.

## Types of Off-Task Actions Noted

Calculate the total number of students engaged in each type of off-task action that you observed during the fifteen time segments. Record each total of off-task actions in the total column.

Analyze the types of off-task actions that you observed:

1. Were students slow to move from one activity to the next?
2. Were students in transition confused about what to do next?

3. Did transition periods lead to discipline problems?

4. Were particular students consistently disruptive?

5. What was the nature of the disruptive activities?

6. Did unoccupied students appear tired, bored, confused?

7. How frequently did students leave the room?

8. Why did students leave the room?

9. How long were students gone from the classroom?

## Types and Quality of On-Task Actions Noted

If you have not already done so, calculate the total number of students engaged in each type of on-task action that you observed during the fifteen time segments. Record each total of on-task actions in the total column.

Analyze the types of on-task actions that you observed:

1. Was the teacher actively involved in questioning and guiding?

2. Did the student-directed groups work productively?

3. Were the individual assignments understood by the students?

4. What type of records did the students attend to?

Next, analyze the quality of the on-task actions you observed:

1. How many students in the teacher-directed group were not attentive and therefore recorded in the unoccupied box?

2. What type of group activities were conducted? Were they meaningful, important, of value?

3. Were the individual assignments of value, important, productive? Were students merely copying or actually working?

4. Were the records kept by the students necessary, of value, important to their progress?

## Number of Students Involved in Each Participation Area

Review the numbers in the total column. Consider the number of students involved in each activity. Analyze the proportion of students in each area.

1. How many students were unoccupied during each time segment?

2. How many students were in transition for each segment and for the total review?

3. How many students left the room during the review period?

4. How many students were involved with recordkeeping?

5. How many students were unoccupied during the review?

## How to Use the Analysis

As you analyze the results of the time-on-task review, you may wish to make some comments at the bottom of the review form. These comments will guide your discussion with the teacher.

Both you and the teacher should sign and keep a copy of the time-on-task review. Your copy will help you to:

1. Review comments and results at a later date
2. Review the data in comparison to other diagnostic data that has been gathered
3. Relate data about student engagement rates to other areas of teacher weaknesses
4. Develop a supervisory action plan
5. Estimate progress at a future time

# PROVIDING FEEDBACK TO THE TEACHER

The results of the time-on-task review should be discussed with the teacher during a conference. It is important for the teacher to know and understand what you have observed.

The conference is an excellent time to isolate actions observed and try to find their causes. Some sample actions and the possible causes for them, that should be discussed with the teacher, are:

| Sample Actions | Possible Causes |
| --- | --- |
| Many students were in transition for long periods of time. | Students may be confused about what and how to move to a new activity. |
| Students sat unoccupied with individual assignments opened on their desks. | Students may not understand the assignment well enough to complete it independenly. |
| Some students in the teacher-directed group paid little or no attention to the lesson. | These students may require a smaller group setting or more attention in the group or better motivation to attend to the lesson. |

Items that require extensive supervisory help should be incorporated into the supervisory action plan. These may include questioning techniques for teacher-directed lessons, meaningful group-directed activities, and motivation techniques.

# Viewing Student Products

Nothing else more accurately confirms what happens in the classroom than student products. These are the results of instruction. They verify what the student has learned, remembered, and incorporated into his or her growing store of information. By collecting and reviewing student products, you can estimate how well students are learning.

## WHY SHOULD STUDENT PRODUCTS BE VIEWED?

There are many objectives to be accomplished by viewing student products. It is possible to assess student growth and development. It is also possible to confirm compliance with district policy in implementing particular curriculum programs. Progress with agreed-upon supervisory plans may also be checked by viewing student products.

There are at least three objectives to be determined by viewing student products. These are: (1) the effectiveness level of instruction, (2) the rate of student progress, and (3) whether district-mandated programs are being implemented.

## Effectiveness Level of Instruction

By viewing student products, you will be able to determine how well students are doing. It is possible to view their products and estimate the progress they have made toward content mastery.

This may be particularly significant when comparing similar classes. The rate of progress in mastery of certain skills between classes of similar levels and student composition reveals important information about the effectiveness of the instruction in each class.

## Rate of Student Progress

Student products will help you determine a progress point in the curriculum for each class. You will be able to look at the topics currently under study and determine the point in the curriculum that has been reached. In this way, you will be able to determine if progress is being made at an appropriate rate.

## Implementation of District-Mandated Programs

By viewing student products you will be able to determine if district-mandated programs have been implemented. Student products should reflect the approach, techniques, and style that are required for particular curriculum areas.

For example, a district that has adopted a particular writing program stressing student motivation and use of creative expression would anticipate a suitable form for teacher correction of student work. That form should avoid the use of red pencil correction by the teacher. Instead, students' written work should be evaluated for creative use of language. A listing of mechanical skills should be recorded separately by the teacher to be used for instruction of the class, groups, and individuals in skills that are not mastered.

If students' work is marked and corrected with a red pencil, you have an excellent indicator that the goals and objectives of the district writing program are not being followed in that class.

As another example, assume that your teachers have agreed upon the policy that written work in all content areas is an objective for the school year for all departments. It is then appropriate to view student products with this objective in mind. Samples of student reports in social studies and science should reflect an emphasis on writing in forms appropriate for those disciplines. When student products do not reflect this objective, you are aware that particular teachers are not working toward a school-wide objective.

## KNOWING WHICH STUDENT PRODUCTS TO REVIEW

Any examples of student work that you consider important are appropriate to be reviewed. These cover the wide spectrum of work that is possible in the classroom.

The following is a partial list of student products that are appropriate for review:

1. **Samples of students' creative written expression.** Review to ensure that students are writing, to evaluate the quality of their written efforts, and/or to monitor a specific writing program.

2. **Class test results.** Review to monitor student mastery of skills, to assess progress through the curriculum, and to judge the level of mastery among students of different abilities.

3. **Homework assignments.** Review to confirm that homework is assigned, to monitor the quality of the assigned homework, and to determine how homework is evaluated.

4. **Classwork samples.** Review to assess the quality of classwork assigned, to determine how classwork is corrected, and to match classwork to teacher plans for instruction.

5. **Unit products.** Review to determine the effectiveness of the unit studied, to view the quality of the products produced, and to assess the diversity of product options open to students.

6. **Written reports.** Review to determine if writing is practiced across the curriculum, and to evaluate the quality of student expression in varied content areas.

7. **Book reports.** Review to confirm that students are encouraged to read, to determine students' opinions of the books they have read, and to assess the quality of the reading materials given to students.

8. **Tapes of students' oral reports.** Review to provide for variety in report possibilities, and to oversee student products in varying forms.

## CRITERIA FOR COLLECTING STUDENT PRODUCTS

The following criteria should be considered as you develop a program for collecting student products.

1. **The availability of your time.** Do not collect products that you do not have the time to review and react to. Every product that is collected must be read and analyzed. In addition, the teacher will expect a response.

2. **Appropriateness of the products.** Certain products are available only at given points in time. These products include: unit projects, summary tests, and so forth. Be sure

that the products you request are available. Other types of products are continuously available. These products include: test results, classwork samples, homework samples, and the like. Products that are continuously available should not be continuously collected.

3. **Standards you have set.** You may have established certain guidelines for viewing student products. For example, you may have requested each class or department to submit student samples of written work each month. It is then important to maintain this guideline.

## FREQUENCY OF COLLECTING STUDENT PRODUCTS

After you have determined which student products you wish to review, determine the time schedule for their collection. Vary both your purpose and time frame to achieve a more comprehensive overview:

| Collection Frequency | Effectiveness |
|---|---|
| once per week | –permits continuous review<br>–time-consuming<br>–appropriate for marginally effective teachers |
| twice per month | –effective for continuous monitoring<br>–time-consuming<br>–most appropriate for small schools |
| once per month | –very effective frequency<br>–vary product requested each month, for example:<br>September – classwork samples<br>October – homework samples<br>November – test papers |
| every other month | –practical for large schools |
| periodic collection of products when they are available | –such products as unit projects, summary tests, book reports, and so forth |

### Rotating Your Collection Schedule

Rotate collection among grades or departments to make the load easier to handle. For example, products due once per month could be collected on different weeks from different grades or departments. For example:

first week    – grades 5 and 6, or English department
second week – grades 3 and 4, or Mathematics department
third week   – grades 1 and 2, or Social Studies department
fourth week – kindergarten, or Science department

## HOW TO RECORD THE DATA FROM
## YOUR REVIEW OF STUDENT PRODUCTS

Student products should be submitted with a top sheet. (See Figure 11-1.) The information completed by the teacher on the top sheet gives you guidelines to use in reviewing the student products.

The teacher should first specify the type of student products that have been submitted. Next, the teacher should state what his or her objective was in requesting this product from the students. The objective should be related to curriculum goals for that subject.

The teacher should then state his or her evaluation of the products that have been submitted. This evaluation should be consistent with the stated objective. Last, the teacher should specify future plans that will be implemented based on the results of the submitted student products.

The top sheet provides space for you to comment after having reviewed the teacher's statements and the students' products.

## HOW TO USE THE DATA AFTER
## REVIEWING STUDENT PRODUCTS

Your review of student products adds to the growing body of diagnostic information about the teacher's effectiveness. You will be able to monitor growth in areas previously identified as well as new needs.

You should keep an annotated copy of the top sheet submitted by the teacher. The original top sheet should be returned with the student products that have been reviewed.

The student product top sheets should be kept sequentially for each teacher. They will enable you to:

1. Refer back to previous top sheets at a later date
2. Evaluate the teacher's growth in particular areas
3. Monitor student progress
4. Compare current comments with those made in the past

Figure 11-1

## TOP SHEET FOR STUDENT PRODUCT REVIEW

Teacher _____ Class _____ Date _____

Product Type:   ____ homework assignment

____ classwork assignment

____ test papers (topic _____)

____ written expression

____ book reports

____ unit projects

____ other _____

Objective: _____

_____

_____

_____

Evaluation: _____

_____

_____

_____

Future Plans: _____

_____

_____

_____

Supervisor's Comments: _____

_____

_____

_____

## PROVIDING FEEDBACK TO THE TEACHER

You should initial, date, and comment directly on the top sheet. Comments may take the form of commendation or suggestions for improvement.

**Sample commendation comments**

1. *"The students have made excellent progress."*
2. *"Your stated objectives have been met."*
3. *"This was a very exciting project."*
4. *"Your future plans show excellent understanding of student needs."*
5. *"The evaluation of the students' work shows insight and concern."*

**Sample suggestion comments**

1. *"How will you use these student results in your plans?"*
2. *"Was your objective clearly understood by the students?"*
3. *"Please see me to discuss the manner in which you correct students' written errors."*
4. *"Have you determined why so many students did not pass the mathematics test?"*
5. *"Would you consider other ways in which reports could be done?"*
6. *"Please see me about the comments you have written on John Hane's paper."*

Observed needs of a more serious nature and ones that require more extensive supervisory assistance may become part of the supervisory action plan. You may find a particular teacher's needs confirmed by several different diagnostic techniques. For example, a teacher's use of mostly lower-level questions may have been observed during informal visits, stated in teacher plans, and written on student test papers.

# Making Formal Exploration Observations

The exploration observation provides the opportunity to gain information about a wide range of teaching skills. It helps you identify areas of the teacher's performance that need improvement and then prioritize those areas for the supervisory action plan.

This observation is dramatically different from guided supervision, which is a learning situation for the teacher. In guided supervision, one area in need of improvement is selected for the focus of the observation. The exploration observation, however, is a diagnostic assessment of the teacher's skills. This assessment may then lead to the identification of the priority area for guided supervision.

An exploration observation is an intense diagnostic assessment and should be used in two circumstances:

1. When little is known about the teacher. The teacher may be new to the school or new to teaching.
2. When the teacher has been identified as marginally competent or close to unsatisfactory. In this case, there are so many areas in need of improvement that the exploration observation is needed to prioritize the supervisory plan.

# THE IMPORTANCE OF MAKING EXPLORATION OBSERVATIONS

The objective of the exploration conference is to conduct a detailed diagnostic assessment of teaching skills. The aspects of teaching reviewed during the observation include the full range of skills required in the delivery of instruction. Other skills involved with organization and management of the classroom may be assessed through an observation of the classroom environment as discussed in Section 9.

The instructional delivery skills assessed in the exploration conference are grouped into three areas: (1) lesson delivery, (2) pupil effectiveness,and (3) teacher performance.

## Lesson Delivery

Before lesson delivery, the teacher prepares the students for instruction by establishing a climate for learning. The teacher quiets the students, gains their attention, and establishes a focus by telling the students what they are going to learn.

Motivation techniques take many forms but should always target the students' understanding of why the lesson is of importance to them. The most effective lesson begins with the teacher's efforts to relate the new material to past student experience or knowledge as a bridge between the known and the unknown.

The delivery sequence starts, when appropriate, with a review of basic skills related to the new concept to be taught. A good presentation sequence presents concrete concepts before abstract ones. This may be accomplished through using manipulative materials first, then visual ones, and oral ones last. In general, concepts that are easy to understand should be presented before more complex ones.

The use of a summary at various stages in the lesson, certainly in the middle and at the end, helps to focus the students on what they have learned, confirm their understanding, and prepare them for what they are about to learn.

Review and reinforcement help to confirm and maintain what has been taught. Review and reinforcement are both immediate and delayed. Immediate review and reinforcement may be practiced as teacher-directed guided practice with the group. Immediate review may be continued as independent seat work. Delayed review and reinforcement usually takes the form of homework or assignments given later in the day or the week.

## Pupil Effectiveness

Lessons that are effective involve the students. They respond to questions and ideas and express themselves freely. The teacher acts as guide and director rather than dominator of the lesson.

Lessons that are appropriate for students contain skills or concepts that are new to the students or those that students have not yet mastered. Students who have gained mastery of a skill or concept should not be involved in a lesson on that topic. It is both boring for the student and a waste of his or her time.

Pupil-effective lessons contribute to the language development skills of the students. This is best done by encouraging the youngsters to speak in complete sentences using correct English.

The most effective lessons are those in which the students speak to and respond to their peers. Their responses should not be constantly directed toward the teacher without consideration for the others who are listening.

Students who display good lesson behavior listen to the comments of their peers and respect their ideas. They wait for an opportunity to speak and offer to help each other..

## Teacher Performance

Questioning technique is a major instructional skill. Good questions are mainly thought-provoking and only occasionally of a factual nature. "Yes" or "no" questions are avoided.

Instructional aids that contribute to the effectiveness of a lesson are multi-modal, appealing to all learning styles. They are prepared in advance and used both appropriately and effectively.

The books, texts, and other written materials used in the lesson must be both appropriate to the content of the lesson and within the level of understanding of the youngsters who will use them.

# HOW TO CONDUCT THE OBSERVATION

Before the exploration observation is conducted, the teacher should be given an opportunity to think through what and how the lesson he or she will demonstrate will be conducted. It is important to give the teacher a format to use in planning and the time to think about the lesson before completing the plan.

## The Pre-Observation Planning Form

The teacher should be given about one week to complete the "Pre-Observation Planning Form." (See Figure 12-1.) The purpose of the form is to give the teacher the specifics of what is expected in the lesson and the opportunity to plan its development.

Figure 12-1

## PRE-OBSERVATION PLANNING FORM

Teacher _____ Class _____ Date _____

Requested observation day _____ time _____

   Approved _____ Alternate day _____ time _____

Subject Area _____ Ability Level _____

Topic _____

Instructional Mode (class/group) _____

Aim _____

_____

State a specific developmental plan for the lesson. Include the motivation, sequence, summary, review, and reinforcement:

_____

_____

_____

_____

_____

_____

_____

_____

_____

_____

_____

_____

_____

Materials / texts / books / instructional aids to be used:

_____

_____

_____

_____

Teacher's Signature

The pre-observation form also serves several purposes for you prior to the observation. First of all, the form will specify the subject, topic, and level of the lesson to be observed. You may wish to specify the subject and the ability level you wish to observe. However, the teacher must select the topic and material appropriate for those students.

The pre-observation form also permits you to make an initial judgment about the specifics that the teacher has planned. By reviewing the pre-observation form, you will be able to evaluate how well the teacher has planned the logistics of the lesson from the motivation to the provision for review and reinforcement.

Since the exploration observation is an assessment rather than a learning experience for the teacher, the pre-observation form should not be discussed with the teacher. How the lesson is planned contributes to the assessment of teacher needs.

The teacher should be consulted to make an appointment for the day and time of the exploration observation. A time that is mutually convenient should be agreed upon. The teacher may make a specific request on the planning form. You must approve that request or suggest an alternate time and date.

## The Observation

Make every effort to be prompt for the observation. When you enter the classroom, greet the teacher and find a place to sit where you can see and hear both the teacher and the students.

You should be prepared with pencil and paper to take notes during the lesson. Verbatim notetaking is the most suitable way to record the lesson as you observe. (See Section 5 for a discussion of verbatim notetaking.) The use of verbatim notetaking will permit you to record exactly what happens during the delivery of instruction. You will be able to record the exact questions that the teacher asks, what is written on the board, and what—as well as how—the students respond.

You will also be able to record what instructional materials are used as well as how they are used. It is important to note how the materials are prepared for their easy and immediate use at the appropriate point in the lesson.

Your immediate impressions should also be recorded so that they are not forgotten. These may include: how an incorrect answer is dealt with, whether all the students are called upon, and how the students treat each other during the lesson.

To assist you in remembering your reactions to the notes you have taken, you may wish to code your notes as you go along. A simple technique is to use a minus sign for items that are not favorable and a plus sign for items that appear to be of good quality.

If the lesson does not include the whole class, it is important to also note what the students not involved in the lesson are doing.

# HOW TO USE THE DATA FROM
# THE EXPLORATION OBSERVATION

Review your verbatim notes as soon as possible after the observation. The longer you wait the less you will remember about what you saw and what you wrote. Notations that are perfectly clear when they were written may be very confusing after a period of time has passed.

Analyze your verbatim notes in comparison to the three skills areas of instructional delivery previously discussed. Group the data as: lesson delivery, pupil effectiveness, and teacher performance.

Look for areas of strength. List these separately. They will be important in preparing your letter for the teacher's file. Next, list the areas of weakness in priority order.

The priority order of skill weaknesses is dependent upon your personal point of view. There are many crucial elements in the delivery of instruction to students. Each part of the lesson contributes to an instructional whole which is effective and efficient. Which of the parts is most important is a subjective decision. It may be most effective to begin guided supervision with the area of greatest interest and concern for you.

It may be helpful, however, to look at areas in need of improvement not in terms of how crucial they are for instruction, but rather, in terms of how easily they can be corrected. For example, using abstract concepts or materials before using concrete concepts or materials is a common error made by teachers. The reversal of presentation to students is easily accomplished. As another example, using immediate review and reinforcement techniques as guided group work is often not done by teachers. This is an easy suggestion for a teacher to implement. Working first on suggestions that are easily implemented and mastered builds teacher confidence and trust.

More difficult skills such as questioning techniques, student motivation, and student involvement will be more effectively worked with after success with initial supervisory suggestions has been achieved. Nothing is more motivating to teacher skill development than the successful implementation of a supervisory suggestion and the delight in observing that the suggestion made a significant difference in teaching effectiveness.

To help you make decisions about crucial areas of teacher skill development, the priority order for those skills, and instructional errors that can easily be corrected, use the "Instructional Delivery Skills Checklist." (See Figure 12-2.) The checklist may be used as a guide while reviewing your observation notes. First, compare your verbatim notes with the checklist. Mark the skills areas that were observed. There is space to comment next to each skill area to qualify your reaction to the observation of each skill.

Next, number or code the skills areas that you thought were weakest. You may well find large differences in presentation even within one skill area. Part of the presentation skill may be excellent. Another part may be very poor. For example, in the

**Figure 12-2**

## INSTRUCTIONAL DELIVERY SKILLS CHECKLIST

| AREAS | COMMENTS |
|---|---|
| **LESSON DELIVERY** | |
| prepares students for instruction | |
| establishes a climate for learning | |
| gains students' attention | |
| states what is to be learned | |
| student motivation | |
| establishes why it is important to learn this | |
| relates new information to prior student experiences | |
| relates new information to prior student knowledge | |
| delivery sequence | |
| reviews necessary basic skills | |
| presents concrete before abstract materials | |
| uses manipulative and visual approaches before oral ones | |
| develops the lesson from easy to complex | |
| summary | |
| medial to indicate where we have come thus far | |
| final to confirm what we have learned | |
| delivered by students, if possible, or by the teacher | |
| review and reinforcement | |
| immediate as guided group work | |
| immediate as independent seat work | |
| delayed as homework assignment | |
| delayed as assignment later that day or week | |
| **PUPIL EFFECTIVENESS** | |
| students' involvement | |
| students respond and contribute freely | |
| teacher does not dominate the lesson | |

| AREAS | COMMENTS |
|---|---|
| **lesson appropriateness** | |
| contains skills new to the students | |
| contains skills not mastered by the students | |
| **language development of the students** | |
| encouraged to speak in complete sentences | |
| encouraged to use correct English | |
| **arrow of recitation** | |
| students speak and respond to the ideas of their peers | |
| students rarely respond only to the teacher | |
| **behavior of the students** | |
| listen to the comments of peers | |
| help each other | |
| wait for an opportunity to respond | |
| **TEACHER PERFORMANCE** | |
| questioning techniques | |
| few lower-level questions are asked | |
| few yes/no questions are asked | |
| mainly thought questions are asked | |
| **instructional aids** | |
| contribute to the effectiveness of the lesson | |
| of multi-modal nature | |
| **books, texts, and other written materials** | |
| appropriate to the content of the lesson | |
| appropriate for the level of understanding of the students | |

area of pupil effectiveness, student involvement and the arrow of recitation may be poor. The other aspects of the area may have been outstanding. The more detailed your analysis of needs, the more effective your supervisory action plan will be.

Last, note the areas of strength. These are important for several reasons: (1) they form the beginning areas to discuss with the teacher, (2) they start the conference on a positive note, and (3) they may be the stimulus for correcting areas of weakness.

## PROVIDING FEEDBACK TO THE TEACHER

Once you have completed your analysis of the observation, you are ready to invite the teacher to a conference. Do not allow too much time to elapse between the observation and the conference. The teacher is understandably concerned about your reactions and impressions. (See Section 21 for suggestions on conducting successful conferences.)

### The Conference

Begin the conference by asking the teacher for his or her ideas about the observation. The insight that the teacher demonstrates will inform you about the teacher's ability to evaluate his or her own performance.

Your discussion with the teacher should always begin on a positive note. Review all the observation items you have coded as satisfactory. At times, this may be difficult. It is always positive to begin by saying that you appreciate the effort the teacher has made in preparing and implementing this lesson.

It is important not to overwhelm the teacher with criticism and suggestions for improvement. Such an overload will serve to create teacher hostility and feelings of despair. Rather, discuss the priority area that you have selected. The depth and intensity of the discussion of that priority area will depend upon how much supervisory work is required.

When the area in need of improvement is easily corrected, or is one on which the teacher can easily focus, the conference will serve as a good opportunity to discuss the item and outline the strategies for correction. When the area in need of improvement requires extensive supervisory help, this conference should set the stage for an intensive guided supervisory action plan.

Rather than discuss the suggestion strategies, the area in need of correction should be discussed and brainstormed with the teacher. Explain how the guided supervisory plan will work and set the next conference date. If the exploration observation has revealed several areas needing improvement, it is wise to inform the teacher that, together, you will focus on other areas in the future.

## The Observation Write-Up

The observaton write-up should confirm what was accomplished during the conference. It should begin with a short summary of the lesson. Next, list the satisfactory or commendable items observed. Then, state the item or related items in need of improvement, noting suggestions for improvement that have been discussed during the conference.

Figure 12-3 shows a sample write-up form for a teacher who *will not* be involved in intensive guided supervision. Figure 12-4 shows a sample write-up form for a teacher who *will* be involved in intensive guided supervision. (See Section 15 for a discussion of intensive guided supervision.)

When there are no satisfactory items to list, thank the teacher for his or her efforts in planning and presenting this lesson. The write-up must include some positive statement even if it is only a recognition of the teacher's performance.

If the teacher will be involved in intensive guided supervision, state the area selected for improvement in the write-up. Instead of making suggestions for improvement, state that the teacher and you have agreed to work together in a guided supervision plan. Put the time and date of the next conference in the write-up.

Suggested comments matched to the instructional delivery skills checklist are given in Figure 12-5. The comments are of both a positive and a negative nature. Negative comments are matched to suggestions for improvement that should be discussed during the conference. Additionally, the comments should be used in the observation write-ups. Both positive and negative comments, with suggestions for improvement, should be used in the write-up shown in Figure 12-3; only positive comments should be used in the write-up shown in Figure 12-4.

**Figure 12-3**

---

## OBSERVATION WRITE-UP

Teacher _____ Class _____ Date _____

**Lesson Summary:**



**Commendable Items:**



**Item(s) in need of improvement/Suggestion(s):**




Sincerely,


_____
Supervisor

**I have read and received a copy of this observation write-up.**


_____
**Teacher's Signature**

---

Figure 12-4

## OBSERVATION WRITE-UP

Teacher _____ Class _____ Date _____

**Lesson Summary:**

**Commendable Items:**

**Guided Supervision Plan:**
As we discussed during the Post-Observation Conference, we have agreed
to work together in a guided supervision plan to improve the area: _____

_____

**Our next conference will be: Date** _____ **Time** _____
**Future areas for guided supervision include:**

**Sincerely,**

_____
**Supervisor**

**I have read and received a copy of this observation write-up.**

_____
**Teacher's Signature**

**Figure 12-5**

## COMMENTS MATCHED TO INSTRUCTIONAL DELIVERY SKILLS CHECKLIST

| Areas for Comments | Comment Type | Sample Comments | Suggestions |
|---|---|---|---|
| 1. Lesson Delivery<br>a. Preparation of students for instruction | Positive | The students were instructed to clear their desks and face the chalkboard.<br>The instructional group was called to the front of the room. | |
| | Negative | Students' desks were filled with unrelated materials that were distracting. | Before the lesson begins, instruct students to clear their desks. |
| b. Student motivation | Positive | The students were motivated using an experience that was well within their understanding. | |
| | Negative | The students were not given any incentive to learn the presented material. | Before the lesson begins, give the students a reason for learning the information to be presented. |
| c. Delivery sequence | Positive | The lesson was developmental, beginning with a review of the facts of five, and moving to the division of a two-place dividend by a five as the divisor, then continuing to the new concept of a three-place dividend. | |
| | Negative | Students were asked to form a generalization before they had been given an opportunity to touch, see, and talk about the materials. | Always present the concrete first, so students can touch and then discuss the topic, before asking for a generalization. |
| d. Summary | Positive | The teacher provided for a medial summary before continuing to the next concept. | |

| Areas for Comments | Comment Type | Sample Comments | Suggestions |
|---|---|---|---|
| | Negative | Neither the students nor the teacher stated a summary at any point in the lesson. | A summary statement of what has been learned helps to focus the students, checks their comprehension of the topic, and prepares them to continue. |
| e. Review and reinforcement | Positive | The class was asked to complete a sample exercise before the lesson continued to the next level of difficulty. | |
| | Negative | When the lesson ended, no follow-up assignment was given. | An immediate follow-up assignment based on the concept taught helps to reinforce the learning. |
| 2. Pupil Effectiveness | | | |
| a. Student involvement | Positive | All students were involved in the lesson. The teacher called on volunteers and nonvolunteers. | |
| | Negative | The teacher did most of the talking during the lesson, allowing little input from the students. | Students learn best when they are actively involved. This is accomplished by soliciting their ideas. |
| b. Lesson appropriateness | Positive | This was a challenging lesson, demanding that students think through past information and apply it to a new situation. | |
| | Negative | The students appeared to know the information that was presented in the lesson. | Check student knowledge before involving them in a lesson. Listening to what they know is not motivating and may be boring them. Try a simple pretest. |

**Figure 12-5 (continued)**

| Areas for Comments | Comment Type | Sample Comments | Suggestions |
|---|---|---|---|
| c. Language development | Positive | The students were encouraged to explain and clarify their answers. | |
| | Negative | The teacher accepted student answers that were stated in phrases or single words. | Help students improve their English by encouraging them to speak in complete sentences. |
| d. Arrow of recitation | Positive | The students spoke to each other rather than directing their comments only to the teacher. | |
| | Negative | The students did not listen to each other. | Encourage the students to listen to each other's comments and statements. You might ask one student to repeat the question or answer given by a peer. |
| 3. Teaching Performance a. Questioning techniques | Positive | The teacher asked a multitude of "why" and "how" questions. | |
| | Negative | The teacher asked mainly "yes" or "no" questions. | Plan the questions you will use before you teach the lesson. Avoid any question that can be answered by "yes" or "no." |
| b. Instructional aids | Positive | The teacher made an appropriate game to be used as a review of the concept taught. | |
| | Negative | The representative material used was too small to be effectively seen by all the students. | If the representative material is not available in a large form, make a transparency and project it. Or, teach the lesson to small groups who can easily see the material. |

# Using Reported Data As an Information Source

Data reported to you is another important source of information about teacher needs. However, this data should be treated with caution because it is secondhand rather than coming directly from your personal observations.

In all cases, reported data should be carefully used, with discrimination and confidentiality. An excellent first reaction is to check validity and reliability.

## WHY SHOULD YOU CONSIDER REPORTED DATA?

Despite your most sincere efforts and dedication, it is not possible to be everywhere at once and see everything. The objective of considering reported data is to be fully informed about what you did *not* see.

Considering reported data also permits different points of view to be expressed. Mistakes can be made, even with the best of intentions, because of hidden or unknown feelings.

## SOURCES OF THE REPORTED DATA

Since the supervisor is open, available, and interested in all points of view and expressions of concern, everything and everyone are potential sources of data. How that data is received and used is up to you.

The following discussion of sources for data includes those that are most typical.

### Receiving Data From Parents

Parents are the most typical of the many sources of reported data. The reports may include both favorable and unfavorable comments about teachers or other staff members. Both kinds of comments must be treated carefully.

In all cases, unfavorable data, usually in the form of a complaint, must be investigated. But there are times when favorable data should also be investigated. For example, Sally's mother tells you how wonderful she thinks Mrs. Jackson is. Sally has told her mother that Mrs. Jackson makes all of the children behave by forcing the "bad" ones to stand facing the wall until they agree to be absolutely silent in the classroom.

Parental reports may involve any member of the staff, from supervisors to teachers to members of the lunchroom staff. The actions of all staff members who are in contact with students are rightly brought to your attention.

Parental reports may be particular in nature, such as, "The teacher will not teach my child how to divide a fraction." Or the reports may be general, such as, "The teacher does not like boys." Some parents' comments are concerned with "... my child." Others talk about "... everyone" or "... all of the youngsters."

### Receiving Data From Teachers

Fellow teachers are another source of reported data. Usually this type of report is a plea for help with a situation that has been going on for a long time. Most teachers will make some attempts to resolve a problem with another teacher before bringing it to your attention. At the point that a teacher complains to you about another teacher, there is usually frustration and anger.

Teachers usually complain about a particular teacher's lack of participation in grade or department responsibilities, which throws all the burden unfairly on others. Lateness or nonattendance at duty station, thus leaving posts uncovered, is another typical teacher concern. The lack of cooperation in sharing scarce materials is still another often-heard complaint.

### Receiving Data From Students

Reported data also comes from students. If students are to believe in you and trust your interest and availability to them, it is important that you listen to them. On the other hand, you must be careful about possible abuse of this avenue of communication.

Some students' reports are real expressions of anger, such as, "The teacher won't let me..." Others demonstrate tearful frustration, such as, "The teacher hates me." Some reports from students take the form of a group action involving many youngsters.

Since students' reports are a sensitive issue and students may be nervous or upset when speaking with you, it's a good idea to ask the student to write you a note about the problem and leave it in your letter box. Assure the student that you will look into the matter as soon as you possibly can.

## Receiving Data From Principals or Supervisors

At times, one of your peers may report the actions of a member of your staff to you. As a professional courtesy, reports of this nature are always taken seriously.

Although reports from your peers in other schools are rare, they do happen. This is especially possible when a parent has two children, one in your school and the other in a different school in the same district. The following episode illustrates the type of teacher report you might receive.

You receive a telephone call from a principal in the district. He or she is very upset and tells you about an incident that just happened with Mrs. Roberto, who has one child in your middle school and one in the principal's elementary school.

Mrs. Roberto went to see the principal of the other school following a conference with a seventh-grade English teacher in your school. Mrs. Roberto's son is in that teacher's third period English class. The teacher told Mrs. Roberto that her son is doing poorly in the area of written expression, and that the reason for his poor performance is probably due to a lack of good instruction in his elementary school. Mrs. Roberto now wants to know what the elementary principal's writing program is all about and how it will be improved to keep her other son, still in the elementary school, from also falling behind.

## Receiving Data From Members of the Community

Community members are a source of reported teacher behavior concerning incidents that occur outside of the school. These types of reports must be treated with courtesy and concern.

Reports from community members are usually concerned with the teachers' lack of supervision during recess periods, student abuse of community property during teacher-conducted walks with the class, poor teacher supervision during dismissal hours, or the lack of supervision on school buses.

# VARIOUS FORMS OF THE REPORTED DATA

Reported data takes various forms. It is a mistake to judge the seriousness of the report according to whether it is written or oral. Some people, who have serious complaints, are not comfortable putting their words in writing. This may be because they do not want a written record to exist, or because their use of English is poor due to limited schooling or foreign language background.

A better indicator of the report's seriousness and validity is the amount of effort involved in bringing the report to your attention. In general, formal reports are far more serious than informal reports.

## Informal Reports

Because you hold a position of public responsibility, informal conversations with community members about school matters can occur virtually any time and any place. School dismissal and early morning line-up are especially "visible" times, when parents or members of the community may stop you to discuss a concern or report an incident.

Every time you are on the street you are open to parent and community discussion and reports. This may happen as you enter the building in the morning or when you leave in the late afternoon. Be prepared to be stopped.

Parent or parent-teacher association meetings are additional times when you are accessible to parents and the community. You may find that there are many people who are anxious to speak with you during the coffee hour. This is a time when open communication is possible and you should make every effort to be available.

District meetings are still another time when you are accessible to your community. At times, individuals may attend these meetings only because they believe you will be there, and they will have the opportunity to speak with you.

## Formal Reports

**Formal Verbal Communications.** These reports are far more serious in nature. The individual who wishes to speak with you makes the effort to find a mutually convenient time to talk or meet with you in private.

One form of formal verbal communication is the telephone appointment. Persons who wish to talk with you may call and ask that you return the call at your convenience. Others may make an appointment to see you in person. These are generally people who are upset and require a face-to-face interview to fully explain the nature of the problem.

Both situations must be taken seriously and given time. It is important to find uninterrupted time to speak with those who wish to talk with you.

**Formal Written Communications.** These reports are, likewise, almost always of a serious nature. Usually, they come from people who are comfortable with the written word and find that means of communication easier.

Formal written communications may take the form of a letter written to the supervisor. Usually the letter contains a serious, personal, and emotional appeal.

At times, formal written communications take the form of a letter to the teacher with a carbon copy to the supervisor. This type of communicator wishes to have an impact on the teacher by ensuring that you are aware of the full intent of the accusation.

## HOW TO USE THE REPORTED DATA

Before using reported data, it is wise to consider three factors: (1) the source of the data, (2) the form of the data, and (3) the content of the data.

Although all reported data must be taken seriously and dealt with, the course of action you pursue, as well as its intensity and promptness, may differ with each report. In general, the content of the report is the most important aspect to consider first.

Reports that deal with mental or physical student abuse, and that come from any source and in whatever form, must be confronted with the greatest possible speed. Regardless of your personal thoughts and opinions on the subject, this type of report must be given prime consideration.

Reports concerned with instruction and learning, from any source, are the next order of importance. Generally, reports that are formal in nature, either written or oral, are taken more seriously than those that are informal.

All other reports that involve teacher attitude, statements, or actions form the third order of priority. Reports from parents, students, and peer teachers are equal in importance. Community reports, while also serious, may not immediately affect school life. Obviously, if you are faced with only one report at a time, that report takes priority.

### Courses of Action

In all cases, regardless of the source, type, or content of the report, you must investigate. This investigation should be appropriate to the reported data, so select the technique(s) that is most appropriate.

**Discuss It With the Source.** The first level of investigation is to discuss the report with the source, the person or persons reporting the data. This is, in fact, accomplished if the report is made in a personal interview with you or during a telephone conversation. If the report is written and sent to you, follow up by contacting the source.

**Discuss It With the Involved Teacher.** The next course of action is to discuss the reported data with the involved teacher. The teacher should be made aware of all of the information you have. At times, the source may ask that you keep his or her name confidential. If this is requested, it is advisable to do so. When it is not possible to fully discuss the report without naming its source, you may want to give the teacher that information. If you believe this may happen, it is wise to tell the source that you will try to maintain his or her confidentiality but that this may not be possible.

The request for confidentiality usually comes from parents who think the involved teacher may take revenge on their child. This fear may be handled by assuring the parents that rather than take revenge, the teacher is more likely to make extra efforts on the child's behalf.

**Observe the Teacher and/or Review Data.** If appropriate, it may be informative to observe the teacher and/or review previously gathered data, such as the teacher's file, observation reports, letters, plans, and conference reports.

You may also want to speak with other individuals who may be involved, such as students, teachers, assistant principals, other supervisors, and so forth.

**Discuss It With Both Involved Persons.** It may be necessary and advisable to hold a face-to-face conference with the source and the involved teacher. This course of action is very useful in determining the degree of validity and reliability of the reported data. A response by the involved teacher to statements made by the source is always more accurate and sometimes more effective than your response can be.

Always be cautious about nondocumented statements from any source, such as "all of the time," "all the students," "everyone says," and the like. These statements should be challenged.


## PROVIDING FEEDBACK TO THE TEACHER

After completing the determined course of action and conducting an investigation, you must come to a conclusion about the validity of the report, the degree of its importance, the need for intervention and change, and the action to be taken.

There are four possible actions to be taken following the investigation of a report. These are:

1. Informal discussion with the teacher
2. Formal discussion with the teacher
3. Formal letter in the teacher's file
4. Involvement with the supervisory action plan


### Informal Discussion With the Teacher

Informal discussion should be held with the involved teacher if you have determined that the cause of the report was an oversensitivity to an issue or a lack of sensitivity to an issue. The teacher should be advised of a more acceptable approach to the issue and a preferred manner of reacting to it in the future.

## Formal Discussion With the Teacher

Formal discussion with the teacher should be conducted if you have determined that the report was the result of inappropriate feelings and attitudes on the part of the teacher. The teacher must be made aware of the unacceptable actions that resulted and be cautioned to modify and control future actions.

## Formal Letter in the Teacher's File

A formal letter is prepared and placed in the teacher's file if the involved teacher is resistant to your suggestions. If this is not the first time that such a problem has been brought to your attention, it is your obligation to write a formal letter making the teacher aware of this and of the fact that future recurrences will not be tolerated.

## Inclusion in the Supervisory Action Plan

If the report is concerned with instruction and the learning process, it may be an appropriate topic for inclusion in the supervisory action plan. Appropriate topics for this action plan include classroom management, organization, and discipline; diagnosis of student needs; individualization of instruction; appropriateness of homework assignments; group instructional techniques; and maximum use of instructional materials.

# How to Match Supervision to Teacher Needs

# Tailoring the Supervision Process to Teacher Needs

Having established both a standard for excellence (see Part I) and a diagnosis of teacher needs (see Part II), you are now ready to make supervision decisions that match supervision to three essential elements:

1. What to work on (the supervisory objective)
2. How to work on it (the supervision plan)
3. For whom (the teacher type)

The use of these elements will make your supervisory efforts both effective and efficient.

## WHY SHOULD YOU MATCH SUPERVISION TO EACH TEACHER?

The issue of differentiation in supervision is complicated by the fact that not only are all teachers different, but even teachers of the same type are not the same. Therefore, they do not profit from identical supervision treatment.

There are two other facts to consider in discussing the need to match supervision to teacher needs. These are: your available supervision time, and teacher preference.

## Tailor Your Supervision Efforts

The identification of teacher needs (discussed in detail in Part II) is the essential consideration in determining what to work on. When diagnosis has been carefully and completely conducted, supervisory efforts can be tailored to the specific skill needs of each teacher.

The identification of teacher type (see Section 4) is the prime consideration in determining how to work on the identified teacher needs. Obviously, success in achieving teacher improvement is enhanced when the way in which you work with that teacher matches the teacher's type.

## Effective Use of Supervision Time

Supervision time, although a priority, is limited and subject to tight restrictions because of the many other demands on your time. That is why efficient use of your supervisory time is essential if effective results are to be accomplished.

For supervision time to be both productively and efficiently used, it must be allocated by need. The question you have to answer is, "How can I achieve the best supervision results for the time I expend?"

This is a difficult question to answer. Consideration must be given to both teacher need for supervision and teacher type. Obviously, teachers with the greatest need for supervision should be given the largest allocation of your supervision time. This group of teachers usually includes those new to teaching as well as those new to your school. Teachers who are marginal in teaching performance or barely satisfactory also fall into this group.

The teachers who require a large amount of supervision time lack many essential teaching skills. In addition, these teachers may demonstrate a low degree of personal involvement in teaching and in the ability to analyze and solve teaching problems.

Teachers with few or no significant skill needs usually require less supervision and therefore less allocated time. However, these better-performing teachers may demonstrate a low degree of ability in the areas of analyzing and solving teaching problems. Therefore, they need supervision time to set them on the solution paths to teaching problems.

Even teachers with no skill needs, who are seekers of perfection in the teaching role, may demand supervision time. These master teachers may prefer working directly with the supervisor to any other supervision plan.

The allocation of your limited supervision time, therefore, is a difficult but important decision. You must balance the greatest need with the anticipated best result.

## Teacher Preference

When drawing up the supervisory objective and supervision plan, it is beneficial to involve teachers in the selection of what to work on and how to conduct that work. Such consideration of teacher preference leads to greater motivation and a commitment to succeed on the part of the teacher.

The conditions under which a teacher should be given either total selection preference, preference to select from among alternatives, a cooperative selection preference, or no selection preference will be discussed.

# WAYS TO SELECT THE SUPERVISORY OBJECTIVE

The selection of a supervisory objective, that is, what to work on, is the result of the diagnosis of teacher needs discussed in Part II.

## Supervisor Selects the Supervisory Objective

You take the lead in identifying supervisory objectives for the teacher who demonstrates many teaching skill needs, especially when these needs are in areas of crucial skills.

When there are many needs in crucial areas, you may need to prioritize the skill areas with which you want the teacher to work. This teacher is given little opportunity to determine what skill needs are included in the supervisory objective.

## Teacher Selects From Supervisor-Stated Alternatives

When the diagnosis of teacher needs reveals several skill needs of equal importance, it is advisable to involve the teacher. After presenting the skill needs that form the supervisory objectives, ask the teacher to select the order in which those skills should be addressed. This involvement of the teacher provides for his or her areas of greatest interest.

Although the teacher selects the order of skills to be addressed, this teacher has little opportunity to determine the specific nature of the skill needs to be addressed.

## Teacher and Supervisor Cooperatively Select

When the diagnosis of teacher needs reveals minor areas in need of teacher skill development, none of which is crucial, both you and the teacher may cooperatively select the supervisory objective. Skill areas in this group include those needing refinement or modification.

Teacher motivation and interest are the prime considerations in achieving skill development. In this case, the teacher selects the supervisory objective with your consent and approval.

## Teacher Selects the Supervisory Objective

When the diagnosis of teacher skill needs reveals few, if any, areas in need of skill development or improvement, let the teacher select the supervisory objective. This selection reflects the teacher's area of interest for professional self-development of new ideas and fresh approaches to instruction, and represents the teacher's personal route on the road to perfection. This approach may be especially effective at the secondary level where teachers consider themselves content experts. Their need to be recognized, admired, and consulted should be acknowledged.

# SELECTING THE CORRECT SUPERVISION PLAN

The selection of the supervision plan, that is, how to work on the objective, is the result of the analysis of teacher type discussed in Section 4. Teacher type involves the degree to which the teacher demonstrates:

1. The ability to analyze and solve instructional problems
2. A personal involvement in teaching

Mastery of teaching skills, the third teacher type area, is not included in the selection of a supervision plan since it is the objective of the diagnosis discussed in Part II and forms the criteria for the selection of the supervisory objective.

## Supervisor-Directed Supervision Plan

You should direct the supervision plan for the teacher type who demonstrates a low to moderate degree of behavior in the areas of personal involvement in teaching and ability to analyze and solve instructional problems. This population of teachers usually includes those new to teaching and those new to your school. Teachers who are marginally effective or barely satisfactory also fall into this population. Excellent teachers who are insecure in some areas and require direct guidance and intervention may be included in this group; it is not their teacher type, but rather their personality, that places them in this group.

The appropriate supervision plan for this group of teachers is intensive guided supervision. Of all the plans suggested, intensive guided supervision requires the most interaction and involvement on your part.

## Supervior and Teacher Cooperatively Directed Supervision Plan

Both you and the teacher cooperatively direct the supervision plan for the teacher type who demonstrates a moderate degree of behavior, with some high degree, in the areas of personal involvement in teaching and ability to analyze and solve instructional problems. This population of teachers usually has a background of successful teaching experience. They are generally highly motivated with good potential to improve their current level of effectiveness.

The appropriate supervision plan for this group of teachers is collaborative supervision, which allows both the supervisor and the teacher to work together and share ideas, suggestions, and results.

## Teacher-Directed Supervision Plan

Here, the teacher directs the supervision plan for the teacher type who demonstrates a mostly high degree of behavior, with some or no moderate degree, in the areas of personal involvement in teaching and ability to analyze and solve instructional problems. This population of teachers usually has a wealth of teaching experience, is self-motivated and truly professional. This group comprises the excellent, outstanding, and master teachers on your staff.

At the elementary level, this group of teachers is easily identified because content expertise is not an issue. This may not be true at the secondary level, however, where content expertise is an area of concern. To achieve a more accurate picture, you may find it helpful to separate the content of what they teach from the instructional approach and personal involvement of how they teach.

There are three supervision plans appropriate for this group of teachers. The selection is a matter of personal preference.

1. Collaborative supervision—The teacher prefers to work cooperatively with the supervisor in developing a supervision plan. This may be especially appropriate at the secondary level if the supervisor and the teacher share an interest and skill in the same content area.

2. Peer supervision—The teacher prefers to work with a fellow teacher in the development of a supervision plan. This plan is extremely beneficial at the secondary level where the division into departments tends to isolate groups of teachers from each other. Bringing teachers from different departments together to work on a common goal will help break down this artificial division. In addition, a significant interdisciplinary approach to

**Figure 14-1**

## SUPERVISION OVERVIEW

| SUPERVISORY OBJECTIVE (What to work on) | WHO SELECTS | SUPERVISION PLAN (How to work on it) | FOR WHOM (Teacher type) |
| --- | --- | --- | --- |
| Numerous critical needs<br>Some critical needs<br>One critical need | Supervisor | Intensive guided | Mostly low degree<br>Some moderate degree |
| Some noncritical needs<br>Refinement needs<br>Modification needs | Supervisor and teacher | Collaborative | Mostly moderate degree<br>Some high degree |
| Minor needs<br>No specific needs<br>Teacher-expressed interest | Teacher | Collaborative<br>Peer<br>Self-directed | Mostly high degree<br>All high degree |

the curriculum may be achieved. The joining of a social studies and an English teacher, for example, may prove very successful.

3. Self-directed supervision—The teacher prefers to work alone in the development of a supervisory objective and the supervision plan. Content experts on the secondary level as well as seekers of new information on the elementary level are particularly suited to this plan.

## INVITING THE TEACHER
## TO PARTICIPATE IN THE PLAN

When you have reached a conclusion about the selection of both the supervisory objective and the supervision plan (see Figure 14-1 for an overview), invite the teacher to a conference. At this conference, the supervisory process begins, with a full discussion with the teacher about both the objective and the plan. (See Section 21 for details on how to conduct successful conferences.)

# Using Intensive Guided Supervision

The intensive guided supervision plan requires your maximum involvement and total control. This plan is, therefore, extremely time-consuming, and it should be undertaken only after careful consideration of the obligations involved.

The plan involves a step-by-step approach to supervision. It begins with the identification of one teacher skill improvement area. The teacher and you then work together to develop a specific and detailed plan for improvement, which is then put into action under your direction and observation. After you have analyzed the results, both you and the teacher confer on the analysis. Those results form the direction for the next step in the process.

As each result identifies a new need or required approach, a specific and detailed plan must be developed, implemented, and analyzed. This process continues in a cycle until such time that both you and the teacher are confident that the targeted skill has been developed and will continue to be practiced. At this point, intensive guided supervision is either dropped for a time, by mutual agreement, or redirected to a new skill target.

# WHICH TEACHERS WILL BENEFIT FROM INTENSIVE GUIDED SUPERVISION?

Intensive guided supervision is a powerful and effective skill development process. A great many teachers, both experienced and skillful as well as those who are inexperienced and lacking skills, can profit from this supervision process.

However, there are three factors to consider when determining which teachers are the most appropriate candidates for the process:

1. The teacher's preference for direct, intense involvement with the supervisor

2. The degree of skill needs that the teacher demonstrates

3. The amount of time that you can devote to this type of supervision process

Although the teacher's preference should be given consideration, it is not the determining factor. Experienced and skillful teachers who prefer your direct and intense involvement may profit from new experiences in other, less direct, supervision plans such as collaboration or a peer process. They may be ready for the next level in professional development.

Some inexperienced and insecure teachers may be fearful about a supervision process which involves you in such an intense analysis of their skills. They may be far more comfortable hiding some of their needs from your review.

The extent of teacher skill needs is a factor that you must determine. This involves consideration of those skill needs in terms of how many, how crucial, and how complex they are. Less experienced teachers usually have more skill needs of a crucial nature that are complex to develop. But, experienced teachers may still have a complex and crucial skill need. For example, an experienced teacher may need help in developing the skills required to work with a new gifted student population in his or her class.

The amount of time you can devote to intensive guided supervision is a personal decision that should be reached realistically. You should consider the scope of your responsibilities and the amount of assistance you can count on. When you can accurately judge the amount of time you can allocate, you will be able to determine how many teachers you can work with in intensive guided supervision. The candidates for this supervision can then be identified.

## Skill Needs

Both experienced and inexperienced teachers with crucial skill needs should be high on your priority list of appropriate candidates. A partial listing of crucial skills follows; you may have others to add. Crucial skills encompass the teacher's ability to:

1. Manage and organize the classroom

2. Discipline effectively

3. Identify instructional skill groups

4. Meet with instructional skill groups while maintaining control over the instruction of students who are working independently

5. Plan and teach a developmental lesson

6. Motivate students with appropriate techniques and strategies

7. Question effectively

8. Involve students in their own instruction

9. Select and use instructional materials

## Ability to Analyze and Solve Teaching Problems

With experience comes, in most cases, the ability to analyze and solve teaching problems. As new teachers gain confidence and face the day-to-day problems of the classroom, they learn how to determine why they have a problem and how to solve it. When an inexperienced teacher is involved in a difficult teaching situation, the development of the ability may lag too far behind the immediate needs.

Even experienced teachers may have difficulty with this ability from time to time. The teaching problem may be new or unusual, or the experienced teacher may be experiencing personal problems that interfere with good performance.

Teachers who demonstrate an inability to analyze and solve teaching problems are important candidates for intensive guided supervision. Here is a partial listing of the causes of this inability:

1. Lack of teaching experience

2. Difficult teaching situation

3. Unusual or complex set of problem causes

4. Insecurity or low self-esteem

5. Disillusionment or depression

## Personal Involvement in Teaching

The teacher with a low personal involvement in teaching is, hopefully, rare. These are the unsatisfactory, marginal, or barely satisfactory members of your staff. This is a most unusual characteristic for new teachers since they are usually excited, motivated, and enthusiastic.

Dealing with low personal involvement is the most difficult supervision challenge since it requires changing an attitude. These candidates are usually not willing to put forth effort. Although success is difficult to achieve in these cases, it is tremendously rewarding.

Teachers who possess low personal involvement in teaching should be considered as appropriate candidates. They demonstrate this low involvement by behavior that includes:

1. Poor attendance record
2. Late arrival and early departure
3. Token attention to school regulations and procedures
4. Token completion of tasks and responsibilities
5. Noninvolvement with professional activities

# HOW INTENSIVE GUIDED SUPERVISION WORKS

The diagnosis of teacher needs, discussed in Part II, should result in the identification of one area of focus for improvement. Now you are ready to begin the intensive guided supervision.

## Pre-Visit Planning Conference

The pre-vsit planning conference involves the six stages of conferencing discussed in Section 21. Specifically, this conference targets:

1. The area of focus for improvement
2. A specific plan to improve this area
3. A rehearsal of the plan
4. The selection of an observation date and time

The area to improve may be selected in several different ways as discussed in Section 14. Who selects the supervisory objective depends upon the areas identified as needing improvement. Consideration must be given to how many areas have been identified and how crucial they are.

The area that becomes the supervisory objective may be selected by:

1. The supervisor
2. The teacher, from among alternatives stated by the supervisor
3. Cooperatively, by the teacher and the supervisor
4. The teacher

Whenever possible, it is advisable to involve the teacher in the selection. Consideration of teacher preference and concerns is a major motivating factor in successful improvement efforts.

Once the area has been selected and confirmed with the teacher, efforts are directed at developing the best plan for improving this area. Since alternative approaches may be acceptable, time should be devoted to exploring various possibilities. This exploration must result in the identification of one specific plan.

The specific details of that plan are now discussed. This should include all aspects of what will be involved, including materials and strategies that the teacher will need to be successful.

It is important to note that the joint planning of the pre-visit conference is markedly different from the "Pre-Observation Planning Form" (refer to Figure 12-1) used for the exploration observation. Since the objective of this conference for intensive guided supervision is improvement of teaching skills rather than identification of needs, your complete participation in guiding and suggesting the plan is necessary.

After the plan has been fully identified and detailed, a rehearsal of the plan may prove most effective. You and the teacher can take various parts in this rehearsal. Your participation as the student(s) may prepare the teacher to effectively deal with responses and/or situations that may arise. Remember, the better prepared the teacher is for the observation, the more successful this phase of the supervision process will be.

When the teacher fully understands and is comfortable with the selected and practiced plan, set a date and time for the observation visit. Consideration of the teacher's preference may have to be modified by your availability.

It is wise to take notes during the pre-visit planning conference so that you will have a written summary of all the aspects of the supervision plan that were discussed, agreed upon, and planned. Both you and the teacher should sign and retain a copy of those notes, which now become your plan specification. (See Figure 15-1.)

## The Visit

It is important to make every effort to be prompt for the scheduled visit. This will help relieve teacher anxiety. After you have entered the classroom, greet the teacher and find a place to sit where you can both see and hear the teacher and the students.

You should be prepared with pencil and paper to take notes during the lesson. Verbatim notetaking (see Section 5) is the most suitable way to record the lesson as you observe.

Verbatim notetaking will enable you to record exactly what teacher and student actions occur related to the area of focus. This form of notetaking will prove valuable in later discussion with the teacher. These notes will also be important in reviewing what actually happened in comparison with the specific plan detailed at the pre-visit planning conference.

Remember that notes taken during the visit should be objective. They should be reflective of teacher actions without evaluation or judgment.

Figure 15-1

**Intensive Guided Supervision**
**Plan Specification**

**Teacher** _____ **Class** _____ **Date** _____

**Supervisory Objective:**



**Plan Specifics:**



**Observation Date:** _____ **Time:** _____



**Supervisor's Signature** _____

**Teacher's Signature** _____

## Post-Visit Analysis

As soon as possible after the visit, take time to review your notes from both the pre-visit planning conference and the visit itself. These are important pieces of information that help you determine how successful the planning and the results are.

Important items to consider in your analysis are:

1. Implementation of the pre-visit plan
2. Aspects of the plan that were not followed, or that failed
3. Observable student reactions to the presented plan
4. Changes in teacher skill in the area of focus

## Post-Visit Conference

When your analysis is complete, the teacher should be invited to a conference. It is wise not to permit too much time to pass between the actual visit and the post-visit conference with the teacher. Not only will you and the teacher have better recall of visitation events, but also prompt scheduling of the post-visit conference will mean less anticipation stress for the teacher.

The teacher should be encouraged, to the greatest possible extent, to present his or her reaction, evaluation, and assessment of the results of the lesson delivered. You should also present your reactions and the reasons for them. If possible, both you and the teacher should reach agreement on the results. When this is not possible, try to achieve a compromise. Always use the exact events and words that you have recorded in your verbatim notes. This is documented data that cannot be disputed.

The purpose of the post-visit conference is to assess how much of the plan was actually achieved. This assessment directs the next step in the intensive guided supervision process. The teacher's skill need is rarely corrected in one visitation cycle. Usually, the post-visit conference becomes the pre-visit planning conference for the next cycle. When time does not permit this to happen, a new pre-visit planning conference is scheduled and the next cycle goes into effect. (See Figure 15-2.)

The intensive guided supervision cycle should continue until both you and the teacher are confident that the desired skill has been developed and will continue to be practiced. Then the supervision plan should focus on a new area of teacher skill need or be dropped for a period of time.

# WRITING THE REVIEW OF THE POST-VISIT CONFERENCE

Your written review of the post-visit conference should confirm what was discussed and agreed upon during the conference. (See Figure 15-3.) Begin the write-

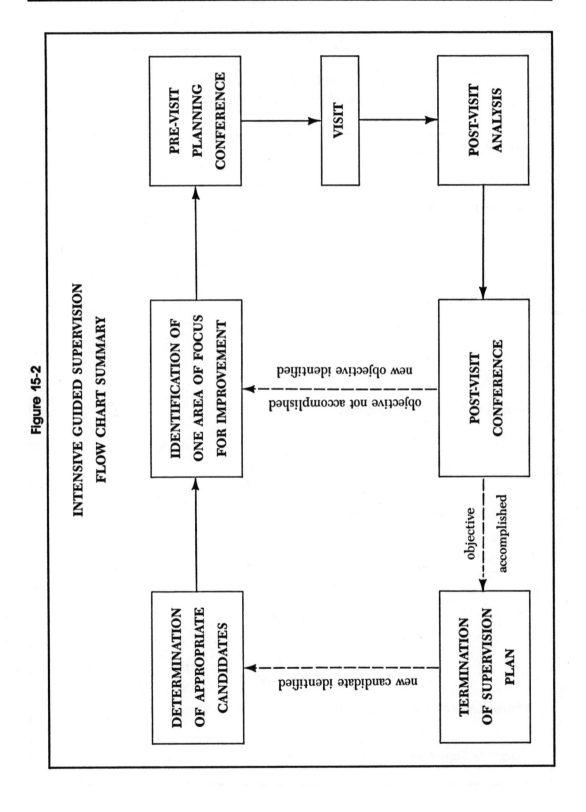

**Figure 15-2**

INTENSIVE GUIDED SUPERVISION
FLOW CHART SUMMARY

Figure 15-3

**Intensive Guided Supervision**
**Review of Post-Visit Conference**

Teacher _____ Class _____ Date _____
Area of Focus:


**Lesson Summary:**


**Commendable Items:**



**Item(s) in Need of Improvement:**



**This supervision cycle has resulted in:**




Sincerely,


_____
Supervisor

**I have read and received a copy of this post-visit review.**


_____
**Teacher's Signature**

up with a statement of the area of focus, followed by a short summary or list of the actions of the teacher and students during the lesson.

Next, list the satisfactory or commendable items or actions related to the area of focus. It is important to let the teacher know what actions were effective. When there are no commendable items to list, thank the teacher for his or her efforts in implementing the planned lesson.

Last, state the items or actions that were not effective. In each case state why these were not effective and how they can be improved. These statements must relate to what was discussed during the post-visit conference. (See Section 12 for a listing of items matched to suggestions for improvement.)

Complete the write-up with a statement anticipating future plans, such as:

1. A statement that this supervisory cycle has been successfully concluded

2. A statement that a new pre-visit plan will be developed

3. A statement that a date has been scheduled for a new pre-visit planning conference

4. A statement that a new area of focus has been or will be selected for the next intensive guided supervision plan

Figure 15-3 shows a sample form for the write-up of a post-visit conference.


# A CASE STUDY OF
# INTENSIVE GUIDED SUPERVISION

Figure 15-4 is a sample case study that shows intensive guided supervision in action. Notes, data, dialogue, and the like, are given.


**Figure 15-4**

---

### INTENSIVE GUIDED SUPERVISION: A CASE STUDY

**Teacher Background:** Graduate of a state-approved teacher training program. This is the first teaching position held.

**Teacher Type:** High degree of personal involvement in teaching is shown by coming to school early and leaving late, and being motivated and enthusiastic. Low degree of ability to analyze and solve instructional problems, probably due to a lack of experience.

**Figure 15-4 (continued)**

**Diagnostic Data Used:**

1. Exploration conference
   a. The teacher expressed a problem related to keeping the students' attention focused during a lesson.

2. Informal visits
   a. Generally, poor student involvement in the teacher-directed lesson.
   b. Questions asked are mostly literal.

3. Formal exploration observation (skill needs identified)
   a. Questioning techniques
   b. Use of representative materials
   c. Motivation techniques

**Supervisory Objective Selected (crucial skill need):**

The improvement of questioning techniques
   a. Eliminate or reduce "yes/no" questions
   b. Eliminate fill-in questions
   c. Eliminate multiple choice questions
   d. Develop critical-thinking questions at the level of analysis, synthesis, and evaluation
   e. Encourage questions that ask how, why, what

**Supervision Plan Selected:** Intensive guided supervision

**Pre-Visit Planning Conference:**

| | |
|---|---|
| **Objective:** | To specify the objective and the plan details for this intensive guided supervision cycle. |
| *Supervisor:* | "At our last conference, you said that you were concerned about the inattentiveness of the students during your lessons. Have you found out why that is happening and solved the problem?" |
| *Teacher:* | "Not really. I keep trying to vary the time of the lesson and the topics as well as the materials I use, but nothing seems to be of much help." |
| *Supervisor:* | "I have been able to see you in active involvement with the students on several occasions. I have made many informal walk-in visits, and we had one exploration observation." |
| *Teacher:* | "Yes, I am aware that you have been observing me. I hope that you have found the reason for the problem." |
| *Supervisor:* | "I believe the problem is related to the types of questions you ask. We began to discuss this topic at our post-observation conference. We will have more time now to fully discuss your questioning techniques. Since our conference, have you had an opportunity to consider the types of questions you ask during a lesson?" |
| *Teacher:* | "I have begun to evaluate my questions, but I really need some help." |

*Supervisor:*  "That is why we are meeting now. Let's talk about some of your questions that I have recorded in my observation notes. Let's discuss them one at a time to discover (1) what they require from the students, (2) why they are not successful, and (3) how to make them better. Let's start with these four questions:
1. The American Indian population in the United States has_____?
2. What caused this? Why did it happen? What are the reasons?
3. Do you think this trend will go up, down, or stay the same?
4. Does the culture of the American Indian contribute to the richness of American culture?"

*Teacher:*  "I think I understand question one. It requires the students to guess the one exact word I want as an answer. The selection of that exact word may be a problem for them. Question four requires a "yes" or "no" answer. I guess that is not a very interesting question. I am not sure what is wrong with the other two questions."

*Supervisor:*  "Question two is composed of three different questions. Students may become confused trying to answer all three since each question may be answered differently. What I think you were doing was trying to improve your question."

*Teacher:*  "You're right. I was not satisfied with the question, so I kept trying to make it better. I would have been better off just waiting for a response and then restating it."

*Supervisor:*  "Question three is a multiple choice question. Why is that not a good type of question to ask in a discussion situation?"

*Teacher:*  "First of all, the students have to remember the question and then the choices of answers. In addition, I am preventing the youngsters from expressing themselves in their own words."

*Supervisor:*  "I am in total agreement with your analysis of the questions. Now, let's discuss how to make all your questions better."

*Teacher:*  "I have been doing some reading about higher order questions. I know that the best route to asking them is to start with why, how, or what."

*Supervisor:*  "That's a good beginning. Also consider this hint. The best questions require students to respond in complete sentences. After we restate your questions, we will plan another lesson. Look at your plans for next week and select a topic that you will teach."

*Teacher:*  "I was planning to introduce the unit on the age of exploration."

*Supervisor:*  "Good, let's spend some time now listing the lesson's objective and the sequence of presentation. Then we will write the questions that you will use in the lesson. After that, we will role play the lesson together."

**The Visit**

**Post-Visit Analysis:**

A review of the verbatim observation notes indicates:

1. An improvement in the teacher's ability to ask questions

Figure 15-4 (continued)

2. Fill-in and multiple choice questions have been eliminated
3. Few "yes/no" questions were asked
4. Many questions began with how, why, what

Considerations:

1. Many questions were at the literal level
2. Many questions required a one-word answer
3. The lesson was planned with my help
4. The teacher must demonstrate the ability to plan and implement a lesson using appropriate questions without help

**Post-Visit Conference:**

**Objective:**    To discuss the evaluation of the classroom observation.

*Supervisor:*  "What is your reaction to the lesson?"

*Teacher:*    "I have some very good feelings about the questions I asked. I was very aware of the quality of each question. Some were very good; others could have been improved."

*Supervisor:*  "Which questions do you think could have been improved?"

*Teacher:*    "The ones that required a one-word answer. They could have been stated in a way to require a whole phrase or sentence as an answer."

*Supervisor:*  "That may have happened because you added some literal questions to the lesson. In any case, you have made good progress in your ability to ask quality questions. I know that you want to be in total control of your ability to ask questions and to evaluate them as they are asked. Do you think you can prepare another lesson, this time by yourself, with a focus on questioning techniques so that we can both evaluate your mastery of that skill?"

*Teacher:*    "I would certainly like to try to do it without help. Will you be able to observe the lesson on Wednesday?"

**The Visit**

**Post-Visit Analysis:**

A review of the verbatim notes indicates:

1. A major improvement in the teacher's ability to ask questions
2. "Yes/no" questions were not asked
3. Multiple-choice questions were not asked
4. Only three of the questions required a one-word answer
5. Most of the questions were at the analysis, synthesis, and evaluation level

Actual questions asked:

1. Why did the story character ...?
2. How would the story change if it were placed in a modern setting?
3. What alternative actions could the family have decided to take?
4. Predict how that alternative action would have changed the outcome.

Considerations:

1. The teacher has achieved a good level of skill in questioning techniques.
2. This supervisory objective will be dropped at this time. Continued progress will be monitored periodically.
3. The new supervisory objective will focus on the original problem, maintaining students' focused attention on the lesson.
4. The teacher will be asked to work on improving one of the following skills— motivation techniques or the use of representative materials.

**Post-Visit Conference:**

*Objective:*    To discuss the evaluation of the classroom observation and plan for a new supervision cycle.

*Supervisor:*   "I know that you feel good about the lesson."

*Teacher:*      "Yes, I certainly do. I have learned so much about asking the best questions possible. I really believe this area is now one of strength for me."

*Supervisor:*   "I agree. You have done exceptionally well with asking questions. It is a difficult area and you have come a very long way in a short time. Let's go back now to the problem you originally stated."

*Teacher:*      "You mean my concern with keeping the students focused on the lesson. There is some improvement. More of the students pay attention more of the time now. Is there anything else I could do to improve that?"

*Supervisor:*   "I think so. There are two areas that could be improved. They will both help you to further improve students' attention. I would like to state both areas for you and ask you to select the one you would like to work on now."

*Teacher:*      "Okay. After my success with questioning techniques, I really have some confidence."

*Supervisor:*   "That's great and very well deserved. The two areas are the use of representative materials and motivation techniques. Which area is of greater interest to you?"

*Teacher:*      "I think I can work on the selection and use of representative materials myself. I am beginning to understand where to go to ask for and find materials."

*Supervisor:*   "Good. I suggest that you ask Mrs. Cooper if you could watch her use materials. You may get some good ideas, as she does that very well."

*Teacher:*      "I'll do that. Therefore, I would like to concentrate my efforts on motivation techniques."

*Supervisor:*   "Let's start to work out ways in which to motivate students at the beginning of a lesson. First, we'll consider some general principles and then we'll apply them to a specific lesson that we will plan together."

**A New Cycle Has Begun ...**

# Working With the Teacher on Collaborative Supervision

The collaborative supervision plan requires the supervisor and the teacher to interact in positive and productive ways. The success of this plan is based on mutual respect, trust, and interest in the professional development of the teacher. Collaborative supervision requires a time commitment but it usually is not as extensive as for intensive guided supervision.

The plan involves a cooperative approach to supervision. It begins with an agreement between you and the teacher about the area to be worked on. The teacher and you then collaborate on the development of a plan and an implementation scheme. The plan is then put into action with or without your active participation, depending upon the implementation scheme. For example, an explicit plan to work with the students to develop a new writing program would involve your active participation in the classroom. However, an explicit plan to improve recordkeeping and management procedures would be tried, refined, and confirmed by the teacher before you were invited to see the results. After the agreed-upon time period has passed, the results of the plan are reviewed by you and the teacher.

The discussion of those results will then determine if additional efforts are to be undertaken, or if the supervision plan has been completed at this point in time. Both you and the teacher collaboratively make that decision.

## DETERMING WHICH TEACHERS WILL BENEFIT FROM COLLABORATIVE SUPERVISION

Collaborative supervision draws its power from the position of respect and esteem in which the teacher is placed. Teachers involved in this type of supervision believe that they are skillful and committed to education. They consider themselves bright and resourceful enough to be cooperatively in control of a supervision plan focused on their professional improvement. These beliefs contribute to the development of confidence and motivation that are characteristic of outstanding teachers.

However, there are three factors to consider when determining which teachers are the most appropriate candidates for the collaborative supervision plan:

1. The teacher's preference for a collaborative involvement with the supervisor
2. The type of skill needs that the teacher demonstrates
3. Your estimate of whether the teacher is sufficiently advanced in professional skills to be able to profit from this type of supervision

The experienced teacher's preference should be given major consideration. These skillful teachers will profit from any of the less direct supervision plans: collaborative, peer, or self-directed. The experienced teacher who selects collaboration prefers to work with you rather than with a peer or by him- or herself. You should assume that the collaborative supervision plan will therefore be the most successful one for that teacher.

On the other hand, the preference of the less experienced or inexperienced teacher for collaborative supervision should be weighed with consideration for the other two factors stated above.

In general, collaborative supervision is not effective for teachers with crucial skill needs. This is because crucial skill needs require intense work over a period of time. In addition, crucial skill needs (whether one, several, or numerous) usually necessitate a guided, step-by-step development of skills. Collaborative supervision is intended to work on noncrucial teacher skill needs. It focuses on the refinement, modification, and enhancement of teaching skills.

In addition, collaborative supervision requires that the teacher bring ideas, suggestions, and experiences to the supervision plan. The teacher and the supervisor share, brainstorm, and collaboratively reach conclusions. The teacher must be capable of this type of participation.

### Skill Needs

Experienced teachers and inexperienced teachers with modification or refinement skill needs are appropriate candidates. An illustrative list of refinement or enhancement skills follows; you may have others to add. Refinement skills encompass the teacher's ability to:

1. Implement a new program
2. Improve discipline techniques
3. Keep more effective records
4. Individualize homework assignments
5. Overcome poor speech habits ("you know," "uh," "okay")
6. Enlarge motivation strategies
7. Encourage student involvement in own instruction
8. Reduce teacher dominance of instruction

## Ability to Analyze and Solve Teaching Problems

Experienced teachers usually demonstrate the ability to analyze and solve teaching problems to a moderate or high degree. It is the difference between the moderate and high degree that usually determines whether the experienced teacher selects collaborative, peer, or self-directed supervision.

The teacher who has a high degree of ability to analyze and solve teaching problems can work effectively on the identification and solution of problems with a colleague or by him- or herself. The teacher who has only a moderate ability in this area needs to interact with you in both analyzing the problems and seeking possible solutions.

It is important to consider teachers who demonstrate only a moderate level of this ability as appropriate candidates for collaborative supervision. Here is a partial listing of the causes for a lack of high ability in this area:

1. Return from a leave of absence
2. Insecurity or low self-esteem
3. Personal problems
4. Some rigidity in thinking
5. Lack of creative insight

## Personal Involvement in Teaching

Experienced teachers who have mastered crucial teaching skills usually demonstrate a moderate to high degree of personal involvement in teaching. The higher the personal involvement in teaching, the better the candidate for any supervisory relationship.

In general, teachers with a moderate to high personal involvement in teaching are good candidates for collaborative supervision. They are professionally dedicated and interested in self-development. They view your involvement with them, in a collaborative supervision plan, as a sincere effort to help them improve.

Teachers who possess a moderate to high personal involvement in teaching demonstrate their involvement by:

1. Spending time on preparation for instruction
2. Arriving early and generally leaving late
3. Taking tasks home to work on
4. Involving themselves in professional discussions
5. Electing to try new materials, ideas, concepts
6. Volunteering for professional committees

# HOW TO USE COLLABORATIVE SUPERVISION

The success of a collaborative supervision plan depends upon the cooperative interaction between the teacher and the supervisor.

## The Planning Conference

The objectives to be accomplished during the planning conference are:

1. To identify the supervisory objective
2. To outline the plan to be implemented
3. To specify the supervisor's involvement
4. To determine a time frame
5. To specify evaluation criteria

Both you and the teacher collaborate in the identification of a supervisory objective. You have the results of various diagnostic activities. The teacher has particular needs and interests. Both points of view must be considered and weighed to make the appropriate selection.

Your diagnostic assessment may have resulted in the identification of particular modification or refinement skills that you believe would be valuable for the teacher. These skills should be presented and explained at the planning conference. If you feel strongly about the value of these skills, you may elect to push for the selection of one of them as the supervisory objective.

The teacher may have a different set of skill needs and interests that are of immediate concern. If the teacher feels strongly about these needs or interests, he or she may push for the selection of one of these areas as the supervisory objective.

When there is a difference of opinion about the nature of the supervisory objective, you should consider which objective, yours or the teacher's, has the best chance for successful implementation. Remember that the single most important factor in the improvement of teacher skills is the teacher's motivation to improve. To continue to press for your objective over the teacher's strongly felt need or interest is poor supervision. Unless you can convince the teacher that your objective will offer appreciably greater benefits to the teacher, delay your selection.

After the supervisory objective has been agreed upon, you and the teacher discuss an appropriate plan. This discussion is characterized by brainstorming—sharing ideas, suggestions, and resources. Alternatives should be explored. The specific plan selected is now recorded in detail. (See Figure 16-1.) All aspects of the plan are stated, including strategies and resources.

The specific involvement of the supervisor is also determined. You may take various roles in the plan. The details of your involvement are recorded and confirmed. Some suggested roles you might take are as:

- **Resource:** to secure materials, make trip arrangements, or arrange for involvement with other personnel
- **Facilitator:** to modify schedules or programs
- **Participant in the plan:** to teach a model lesson
- **Active observer in the plan:** to interact with the teacher
- **Passive observer in the plan:** to watch teacher actions

A time frame for the expected completion of the plan should be set and recorded. The time frame may be modified at a future date, but specific actions are more likely to take place when they have a specified date.

Finally, determine how the results of the plan will be evaluated. The form of the evaluation should fit the plan to be implemented. Evaluation criteria include:

1. Observation of student actions
2. Observation of student products
3. Observation of teacher actions
4. Conference between the supervisor and the teacher
5. Comments of parents
6. Comments of other teachers
7. Written presentation of the plan's results

## Monitoring the Plan

Your first obligation in the collaborative supervision plan is to fulfill your role commitment. Whatever action and involvement have been specified must be com-

Figure 16-1

## Collaborative Supervision
## Plan Specification

Teacher _____ Class _____ Date _____

**Supervisory Objective:**



**Plan Specifics:**




**Supervisor's Involvement:**




**Time Frame:**


**Evaluation Criteria:**




Supervisor's Signature _____

Teacher's Signature _____

pleted by you as soon as possible. Your actions or inactions are related to the success or failure of the supervision plan.

You must be aware of the time frame set and the amount of time that has passed. Rather than wait until the specified time has passed to check with the teacher, check periodically along the way to remind, encourage, and ensure that the teacher is progressing with the specified plan. Periodic checks include:

1. Inspection of teacher plans
2. Short notes sent to the teacher
3. Informal visits
4. Informal review of student notebooks

If the plan is proceeding as specified, no further action is necessary. However, if the plan is delayed, in trouble, stalled, or inoperative you must intervene. It is important to determine exactly what is happening, or not happening, and why. Intervention actions include:

1. A conference with the teacher
2. Informal observations
3. Formal review of student products

Your intervention actions will provide important information. You will then be able to make a decision about the future of the collaborative supervision plan. These decisions include whether:

1. The plan is proceeding in a positive way
2. Additional resource needs must be met
3. The teacher must be consulted because action should be taken to modify or change the plan, suggest alternative actions, or cancel the plan and prepare for a new supervision plan

## The Evaluation

The specifics of the planned evaluation strategies should be completed by the agreed-upon date. The date may be flexible to provide for unforeseen events such as teacher absence, snow days, district priorities, and so forth. A new evaluation date may be set.

The agreed-upon evaluation criteria should be collaboratively reviewed with the teacher. Both you and the teacher should analyze the results and come to an agreement about the success of the collaborative plan. At that point, you should determine, together, if further action is needed on the supervision plan. If this is the case, a new or modified objective may be set. This new or modified objective must be matched to a specified plan, the supervisor's involvement, a time frame, and evaluation criteria.

Figure 16-2

**Collaborative Supervision
Plan Review**

Teacher _____ Class _____ Date _____

**Supervisory Objective: (accomplished totally/partially/not at all)**

**Plan Specifics: (implemented successfully/unsuccessfully/not implemented)**

**Evaluation Criteria: (high / moderate / low success degree)**

**Time Frame:**

**Future Supervision Plan:**

Supervisor's Signature _____

Teacher's Signature _____

If both you and the teacher agree that the collaborative plan has been successfully met and no new immediate needs are apparent, the supervision plan is terminated.

## WRITING YOUR REVIEW OF THE COLLABORATIVE SUPERVISION

Your written review of collaborative supervision should confirm what was discussed and agreed upon during the review of the evaluation strategies. (See Figure 16-2.) Begin by stating the supervisory objective, and note whether it was accomplished totally, partially, or not at all. Next, list the plan specifics and whether they were implemented successfully, unsuccessfully, or not implemented. Then specify the evaluation criteria, noting the degree of success. The actual time frame used should be stated. Last, state whether there is a future supervision plan that has been mutually agreed upon. If a new collaborative supervision plan has been agreed upon, the statement should be followed by, "See the plan specification dated..." If the supervision plan has been terminated, this should also be stated. Both you and the teacher should sign the write-up.

## A CASE STUDY OF COLLABORATIVE SUPERVISION

Figure 16-3 is a sample case study that shows collaborative supervision in action. Notes, data, dialogue, and the like, are given.

### Figure 16-3

---

**COLLABORATIVE SUPERVISION: A CASE STUDY**

**Teacher Background:** Ten years of successful teaching experience.

**Teacher Type:** High degree of personal involvement in teaching is shown by coming to school early and leaving late, being motivated and enthusiastic, and being a respected and accepted member of the professional staff. Moderate degree of ability to analyze and solve instructional problems is shown by the inability to see beyond the obvious, a lack of self-confidence, and a lack of imagination and creativity.

**Diagnostic Data Used:**

1. Exploration conference
   a. The teacher expressed an interest in developing a problem-solving student council.

2. Informal visits
   a. Students are generally on-task.
   b. Good control of student behavior.

3. Teacher plan review
   a. Area of writing poorly explained or specifically described.

4. Student products review
   a. Student writing efforts are generally of poor quality.
   b. Teacher uses unacceptable strategies for evaluation, instructional planning, and communication to students.

**Supervisory Objective Desired by the Supervisor (refinement need):**

The improvement of the writing program
   a. Motivation techniques
   b. Peer suggestions for improvement of both content and structure
   c. Student rewriting efforts
   d. Teacher evaluation (comments on content with positive suggestions, and separate listing of structural needs for groups or individual improvement)

**Supervision Plan Selected:** Collaborative supervision

**Planning Conference:**

**Objective:** To specify the details of a collaborative supervision plan.

*Supervisor:* "The last time we spoke, you expressed areas of interest and concern. Have you had an opportunity to reflect on those ideas?"

*Teacher:* "Well, I have given some of my ideas some thought, but I must say I am not ready with a fully developed plan."

*Supervisor:* "Would you be interested in discussing a different idea for a supervision plan at this time?"

*Teacher:* "Of course. I am interested in hearing what you have been thinking about."

*Supervisor:* "I am concerned about your writing program. I think that we can work together to improve what you are doing and bring it more in line with your interest in student self-development."

*Teacher:* "I am not pleased with my writing program, and I know that it can be improved. What did you have in mind?"

*Supervisor:* "I would like to work with you to implement a peer review and improvement approach to student writing."

**Figure 16-3 (continued)**

*Teacher:* "I am very interested in doing that. How does it work?"

*Supervisor:* "Let's plan it out. First, the group should have a common experience about which to write. Next, each student writes a piece about the experience. Then small groups of five or six students meet. The groups are given specific guidelines for listening and reacting to the work of their peers."

*Teacher:* "Perhaps a class trip might provide a common experience about which to write."

*Supervisor:* "Yes, that is a very good idea. Can I be of help in planning that trip?"

*Teacher:* "You can. I would like to take a trip as soon as possible. Can you help me secure a bus on such short notice?"

*Supervisor:* "I certainly will try. Let me know when the trip will be and the site as soon as possible."

*Teacher:* "I'll make that decision by tomorrow. Now I would like to focus on some of the other ideas you gave me. Do you think it advisable to give the students a list of what to look for and observe during the trip to give them some information about which to write?"

*Supervisor:* "That sounds like a very good idea."

*Teacher:* "I would like to work out all of the details. I am very interested in this idea."

*Supervisor:* "Good, then let's make some plans. Our supervisory objective will focus on the writing program. Let's outline the plan that you will work out."

*Teacher:* "The plan will begin with a trip. The students will have a set of questions to answer while making the visit. The objective of the questions is to provide them with information. After the trip, the class will have one week to complete a composition about the trip. I will then have a class lesson about guidelines for listening and reacting to students' compositions. Could you give me some suggestions for those guidelines?"

*Supervisor:* "In general, the guidelines would include that they listen attentively while the author reads his or her composition. The group should then ask the author specific questions to clarify what they heard, such as, 'Did you tell me everything you can about where you were? How things looked? What you liked or did not like? Why you liked or did not like what you saw?' And so on. In general, the group should aim at clarification of what the author stated. The author takes notes about the suggestions that the group makes. There are many ideas in the writing program manual that was distributed last September. Select a set of listening and reacting guidelines that fit the subject of your writing topic."

*Teacher:* "I have the manual. I will refer to it for the guidelines. Will you help me introduce these ideas to the class? I would like you to develop them with me."

*Supervisor:* "Yes, I will do that. When will you be ready to teach that lesson?"

*Teacher:* "I think I can give the class the guidelines for the trip. So, let's plan that class lesson for one week after the trip, when the compositions will be due."

*Supervisor:* "Fine, we will set that cooperative lesson as soon as the class trip is arranged. Now let's set the time frame for this collaborative supervision cycle."

*Teacher:* "I would think that we should see some results within two weeks after the trip."

*Supervisor:* "Good. Next, we must discuss how you will evaluate the results of the students' rewritten compositions following the groups' reactions to the content and the structure."

*Teacher:* "I would like to make another date with you to discuss that. Could we plan to do that next week?"

*Supervisor:* "Fine. How about next Wednesday at 10:30?"

*Teacher:* "I'll be ready by then. It will give me a chance to review the writing program manual."

*Supervisor:* "That sounds very good. Now, there is one last point to be considered. That is, what evaluation criteria should we use to judge the students' writing progress?"

*Teacher:* "The best criteria, of course, is their writing efforts following the group reaction to their first draft. It would be helpful to me if the evaluation was of my evaluation of their rewritten compositions following the group reactions."

*Supervisor:* "That is perfect. We will then be able to determine how the students' writing efforts have improved through a common experience and a group reaction to both the content and structure of their writing. Your evaluation can take their past performance into account."

*Teacher:* "I am looking forward to this new approach. It is very interesting and challenging."

*Supervisor:* "Let's clarify now what our objective is, the plan we have outlined, how I will collaborate with you in the plan, the time frame we expect to need, and the evaluation criteria that we have specified. In addition, let's both note the date and time of our next meeting targeted at discussing your evaluation of students' written work."

**Second Planning Conference:**

**Objective:**    To specify a procedure for evaluating students' written work.

*Teacher:* "I have read the writing manual you discussed at our last conference and I think I understand how students' written work should be evaluated. But, I have a few questions about that process."

*Supervisor:* "Let's start with your questions."

*Teacher:* "The manual is very explicit about avoiding red pencil corrections on students' compositions. Only comments about the content of the work should be recorded. How, then, will students know they made structural mistakes?"

**Figure 16-3 (continued)**

*Supervisor:* "Let me begin to answer by asking you a question. Have you ever corrected a student's composition in detail and then asked the student to rewrite the composition only to find that the student rewrites most of the same errors even with the corrections in front of him or her?"

*Teacher:* "That has happened to me any number of times. Are you saying, then, that students do not see or understand their errors if the corrections are done for them?"

*Supervisor:* "Yes, that is exactly what I am saying and something else also. How do you think a student feels about a piece of his or her work being returned with red marks all over the page?"

*Teacher:* "I know those marks make the students feel awful. One student actually told me she thought that what she had to say in her writing was not important to me because all I seemed to care about was her spelling and grammar."

*Supervisor:* "That is what we want to stop doing. We want the students to feel that what they have to say is very important."

*Teacher:* "That's fine and I agree, but how can we get them to write using good English? I know the manual talks about teacher listing of student skill needs. Lessons on those skill needs should then be taught to groups, individuals, or the whole class. But how can I show them the errors in their written work?"

*Supervisor:* "You might list, at the bottom of their compositions, the errors you found in their writing. For example, you might list spelling, quotation marks, commas. The students are asked to reread their compositions to find those errors and correct them on the same page. You then review the corrected work."

*Teacher:* "That's fine for some students, but others will never be able to find, let alone correct, their errors. What do I do with them?"

*Supervisor:* "There are several ways to deal with those students. One way is to 'buddy' the student with a good writer. Have them work together to find the errors and correct them. Or, you might meet with the student individually and work through that composition together, helping him or her find the errors. Remember that you will also be teaching lessons in needed skills. Hopefully, those lessons will also help."

*Teacher:* "I think I will try a combination of those ideas. I would like to see what works for my students."

*Supervisor:* "Fine. Keep me posted on how it works."

**Monitor Activities:**

1. A trip permission form was submitted.
2. Guidelines for trip observations were included in the teacher plans.
3. The trip was taken on schedule.
4. The teacher made an appointment with the supervisor to cooperatively teach a class lesson on guidelines for listening and reacting to the written work of class peers.
5. Informal visits to the classroom were made to see writing efforts and hear student reaction sessions.

**Evaluation:** Students' rewritten compositions with the teacher's evaluation are submitted within the specified time frame of two weeks.

**Plan Evaluation Conference:**

**Objective:**    To discuss the results of the supervision plan.

*Supervisor:*    "What do you think of the results of the new writing process?"

*Teacher:*    "Frankly, I am surprised. I did not expect to get such good results. I am also delighted by the students' new interest and excitement in writing."

*Supervisor:*    "I am really glad that it seems to be working. What specifically have you found?"

*Teacher:*    "The youngsters are beginning to be able to help each other correct, improve, and refine their work. There are some good human relations interactions happening. More work is needed, however, because the students need additional experiences to really be able to do this well."

*Supervisor:*    "Are you planning to give them those experiences?"

*Teacher:*    "Definitely. I will use the peer review process for all written work. I have also started the small group instruction of needed skills. It will take time to determine if the skills lessons have an impact on the actual writing."

*Supervisor:*    "I saw your evaluation of the students' papers. You really did a fine job. No red corrections. Instead, you listed areas of need on the bottom and commented on the content. Your top sheet listed the students who need specific skills."

*Teacher:*    "The students liked the new evaluation. When you return the set of papers to me, I will put the students to work on finding their errors."

*Supervisor:*    "You seem to be very encouraged by this first attempt."

*Teacher:*    "Yes, I am. The writing is better, much better, and their attitude about writing is wonderful. But both the students and I have a long way to go yet in refining this new approach."

*Supervisor:*    "Would you like to work through a second collaborative supervision plan on the same topic?"

*Teacher:*    "That would be helpful. I have some ideas about how I would like to approach the next writing effort."

*Supervisor:*    "Fine. Let's start to plan it out."

**A New Cycle Has Begun ...**

# Considering Peer Supervision

A peer supervision plan takes the control of supervision out of the supervisor's hands and places it in the hands of the two teachers who will work together. The success of the plan is dependent on the interaction between these two teachers. Therefore, a peer supervision plan should be considered only if you have total confidence in the participating teachers.

Peer supervision may be the suggestion of two teachers who wish to work together on a task of mutual interest. For example, both teachers may be interested in increasing student involvement in teacher-directed lessons. Or, you may make the suggestion to two teachers who would be appropriate candidates to work on a school project or problem. For example, you may wish to ask two teachers to work together to develop an implementation model for a new district curriculum.

Teachers involved in peer supervision jointly agree on a supervisory objective, an explicit plan, evaluation criteria, a time frame, and a means of reporting to you. The teachers' report should include a recommendation based on the results. The recommendation may be to conclude the peer supervision efforts since the objective has been met. Or, the recommendation may be to continue the supervision plan since more work is needed.

## WHO WILL BE HELPED BY PEER SUPERVISION?

Peer supervision provides teachers the opportunity to supervise themselves. Teachers who are involved in a peer supervision plan are at the top of their profession. They are considered excellent, outstanding, and master teachers. It is their professional skill that directs them to constantly seek to improve, refine, and create for the profession.

Peer supervision recognizes this skill and places the teacher in a position of importance. It is an excellent way to keep motivation and self-development at a high level for these master teachers. In essence, peer supervision places further professional development in the hands of the master teacher.

It is therefore very important to use care when selecting appropriate candidates for this supervision plan. The following factors should be given careful consideration:

1. The teacher's ability to observe, analyze, and share constructive suggestions with a peer

2. The teacher's desire to work with a peer in this type of relationship

3. A professional attitude about teaching as the most important career

4. Professional knowledge and understanding of new ideas and approaches

5. An interest in working on the identified area

Teachers working in a peer supervision plan should possess, or be interested in developing, observation and analysis skills. Some teachers naturally possess the ability to analyze what they do as well as what they see others do. Other teachers need some assistance in developing these skills. Your major role in this supervision plan, when tried for the first time, is to help the teachers develop the necessary skills.

Peer supervision should involve only those teachers who wish to work together. In general, teachers who do not get along well for whatever reasons should not be paired for peer supervision. The result of such a union may well be increased hostility. On the other hand, teachers who are close personal friends should also not be paired for peer supervision. Close friends may have problems with criticizing each other. If no constructive criticism takes place, little professional growth can take place. The best peer grouping for this supervision plan is between teachers who have a positive professional relationship. The teachers should have mutual respect and appreciation of each other's work.

Since peer supervision is self-directed, it should involve only those teachers with a professional attitude about teaching. They should both enjoy and be dedicated to the profession. This attitude promotes an intrinsic desire to improve without outside influence.

Teachers in a peer supervision plan should have professional knowledge and understanding of current and experimental teaching strategies. These are the "idea people" who constantly seek new information. The information is then viewed in terms of how this new strategy would fit the instructional situation in their class or school. These teachers are willing to take the risk of trying something new.

Of course, the teachers involved in a peer supervision plan must agree on the supervisory objective. It is therefore essential that both teachers are interested in working on the stated objective.

## Skill Needs

Master teachers with an interest in self-development and/or refinement of teaching strategies, techniques, and curriculum are appropriate candidates. A suggested list of refinement and self-development skills possessed by the master teacher follows; you may have others to add. The master teacher should have the ability to:

1. Create instructional materials
2. Create instructional strategies
3. Develop new curriculum or courses of study
4. Develop interdisciplinary areas of study
5. Encourage student involvement in own instruction

## Ability to Analyze and Solve Teaching Problems

One of the qualities of the outstanding or master teacher is the ability to recognize that there is a problem, analyze the problem, and then find a way to solve it. The master teacher does this without help. That is why these teachers are especially suited to selecting their supervisory objective and then working on it.

## Personal Involvement in Teaching

Outstanding and master teachers demonstrate a high degree of personal involvement in teaching. To these teachers, teaching is the most important of all professions. Because their efforts at self-development are sincere and of importance to them, a peer supervision plan is a good choice. These teachers are capable of carrying the burden of responsibility demanded by the supervision plan.

Teachers who possess a high degree of personal involvement in teaching demonstrate their involvement by:

1. Taking professional development courses
2. Attending conventions, lectures

3. Reading extensively in the field

4. Involving themselves in professional discussions

5. Designing, creating, and using new materials, ideas, and concepts

6. Volunteering for professional committees

7. Earning the respect and admiration of their peers

8. Being considered star members of the staff

# THE STEPS TO FOLLOW IN PEER SUPERVISION

The success of a peer supervision plan depends upon the professional interaction between two teachers working on an objective of mutual interest and need.

## The Planning Conference

The teachers involved in peer supervision should accomplish the following objectives during the planning conference. You should confirm that all five objectives are met. The objectives are:

1. To identify the supervisory objective

2. To outline the plan to be implemented

3. To determine an appropriate time frame

4. To specify evaluation criteria

5. To state that the results of the supervisory efforts will be reported to the supervisor

The objective for the supervisory effort may come from two different sources. It may come from the involved teachers or from the supervisor. Objectives that come from the involved teachers are specific to the individual needs and interests of those teachers. Two teachers may wish to join efforts to work on a problem, area of interest, or a new strategy. Having made this decision, the teachers would then make an appointment to see you to discuss the objective.

Objectives that come from the supervisor address the interests and needs of a grade, a department, the school, or a district-wide concern. Having identified this interest or need, you would seek teachers who may be interested in working together to find solutions or design models. Those teachers are called to a planning conference for the purpose of presenting the objective. The teachers should feel equally comfortable with accepting or rejecting the suggested objective.

Once the supervisory objective has been identified and the teachers have agreed to a peer approach, the work plan is outlined. (See Figure 17-1.) Those teachers who

## Figure 17-1

**Peer Supervision
Plan Specification**

Teacher _____ Class _____ Date _____
Teacher _____ Class _____ Date _____

**Supervisory Objective:**

**Plan Specifics:**

**Time Frame:**                    **Modification:**

**Evaluation Criteria:**

**The results of the plan will be reported to the supervisor within the time frame.**

Supervisor's Signature _____

Teacher's Signature _____

Teacher's Signature _____

identified the objective and then brought it to you may have also discussed and outlined a suggested plan. The plan is then reviewed with you.

Teachers who have come at your request to listen to a suggested objective may use the planning conference to brainstorm a plan outline. In both cases, when the plan is brought to you or when the plan is developed at the planning conference, your participation should be minimal. Peer supervision capitalizes on the experience, skill, creativity, imagination, and magic of the experienced teacher. Your participation in the development of a plan should be limited to providing needed information, resources, and support assistance.

The teachers must identify an appropriate time frame for the peer supervision plan. The time frame should be flexible to provide for unforeseen constraints and problems that may arise. If the time frame is modified at a later date, the teachers should notify you.

The evaluation criteria specified by the teachers are the desired results of the peer supervision plan. These results should relate directly to the original objective set. The results may be demonstrated in a variety of ways and the involved teachers should agree on the ways in which they wish to demonstrate them. Evaluation criteria may include:

1. Observation of student actions

2. Observation of student products

3. Teacher production of a product

4. Teacher demonstration for other teachers

## The Supervisor's Role

Your most important role in peer supervision is to assist the teachers in gaining the skills they do not have but may need to complete the supervisory objective. For example, if the teachers are working together to design a new curriculum, you may wish to meet with them to discuss the components and structure of a curriculum. The teachers may request an existing curriculum manual to use as a model.

When the peer supervision plan involves teacher observations, you should hold a meeting with the teachers to discuss observation techniques and recording hints. It may be helpful to model these observation skills for both teachers while observing someone else. Or, model the observation skills with each teacher individually as you observe the peer teacher together. Remember, it is not necessary for the teachers to be perfect at observation skills for them to be able to help each other work on a specific aspect of teaching. The teachers will gain skill as they continue to watch each other perform.

A second important aspect of your role in this supervision process is to provide the participating teachers with as much additional working time as possible. This time will be needed by the teachers to confer following the observations, to discuss rough drafts that have been written, or to discuss strategies that have been tried.

## Monitoring the Involved Teachers

The teachers' work on the peer supervision plan is confidential. Observation notes, feedback conferences, rough drafts, and the like, are shared only with the involved teachers. You should not request such information unless your participation is solicited by the teachers.

Your role is to encourage and reassure the teachers' efforts and reaffirm your continued interest. Progress on the plan may be determined through informal dialogue about how things are going. Be sure to clarify that you are available at any time for any purpose if requested.

## The Evaluation

The plan evaluation should be presented to you by both of the teachers within the specified time frame. If more time is required, you must be notifed in writing and the plan specification changed. If the teachers have not requested a plan evaluation conference by the time specified, you should arrange the conference.

The agreed-upon evaluation criteria should be reviewed by you and the involved teachers. You and the teachers analyze the results and come to an agreement about the level of success that has been achieved. There should be agreement about the need to continue the plan or terminate it. If the teachers express a desire to continue working together to further develop the plan, the original plan specification should be examined. If that plan specification is still appropriate, then a new time frame should be set. If the plan is no longer appropriate, it should be modified or rewritten.

## YOUR REVIEW OF PEER SUPERVISION

Your written review of peer supervision serves to confirm what was discussed during the review of the evaluation strategies. (See Figure 17-2.) Note whether the supervisory objective has been accomplished totally, partially, or not at all. Then detail the degree to which the plan specifics were followed and achieved: successfully, unsuccessfully, or not implemented. Review the evaluation criteria and state the degree of their success. The actual time frame used should be recorded. Last, detail whether there is a need to continue the supervision plan, change the plan specification, or terminate the plan.

Figure 17-2

## Peer Supervision
## Plan Review

Teacher _____ Class _____ Date _____
Teacher _____ Class _____ Date _____

**Supervisory Objective: (accomplished totally / partially / not at all)**

**Plan Specifics: (implemented successfully / unsuccessfully / not implemented)**

**Evaluation Criteria: (high / moderate / low success degree)**

**Time Frame:**

**Future Supervision Plan:**

**Supervisor's Signature** _____

**Teacher's Signature** _____

**Teacher's Signature** _____

# A CASE STUDY OF PEER SUPERVISION

Figure 17-3 is a sample case study that shows peer supervision in action. Notes, data, dialogue, and the like, are given.

## Figure 17-3

### PEER SUPERVISION: A CASE STUDY

**Teacher Background:** Teacher A has been a successful and respected teacher for twelve years. Teacher B has had a record of successful teaching experience for more than ten years.

**Teacher Type:** Both teachers have a high degree of personal involvement in teaching, as shown by their coming to school early and leaving late, being motivated and enthusiastic, and being respected and acknowledged as superior teachers by the staff. Both teachers have a proven high degree of ability to analyze and solve teaching problems, as shown by their ability to see beyond the obvious, their self-confidence, and their imagination and creativity.

**Diagnostic Data Used:**

1. Exploration conference
   a. Teacher A has expressed an interest in integrating learning experiences in more than one subject area.
   b. Teacher B has expressed an interest in incorporating citizenship concepts in the social studies and language arts areas of the curriculum.

2. Informal visits
   a. Teacher A has the students on-task and demonstrates good control and management of the learning environment.
   b. Teacher B's students are self-directed and in control of the instructional requirements made of them; they demonstrate excellent management techniques related to their learning.

3. Teacher plan review
   a. Teacher A's plans are detailed and specific concerning the objectives, strategies, and materials to be used.
   b. Teacher B's plans are carefully prepared with specific details of all aspects of the instructional strategies to be implemented.

4. Student products review
   a. Teacher A's student products are prepared with care and concern.
   b. Teacher B's student products demonstrate pride and excitement in the learning process.

**Supervisory Objective Suggested by the Two Teachers (refinement need):**

The development of an interdisciplinary approach to instruction in the American governmental process.

**Supervision Plan Selected:** Peer supervision

**Planning Conference:**

**Objective:**  To specify the details of a peer supervision plan.

*Supervisor:*  "I have been looking forward to this meeting with great interest. Your conference request note stated that you were interested in discussing a peer supervision objective."

*Teacher A:*  "That's correct. We have been talking about this area of interest for some time, and now we are ready to present it to you."

*Teacher B:*  "We think this mutual work will benefit many teachers who may be interested in the subject."

*Supervisor:*  "What is the objective you wish to accomplish in your peer supervision plan?"

*Teacher A:*  "We wish to write an interdisciplinary curriculum for the study of the process of American government."

*Teacher B:*  "We think this subject is really not covered, or not adequately covered, in the current curriculum."

*Teacher A:*  "Few, if any, of our students are aware of how their government is organized and how it works. That is valuable information for everyone."

*Supervisor:*  "I agree. The topic is important. How will you find time in an already crowded curriculum?"

*Teacher B:*  "That is why we believe our plan is so powerful. Rather than isolate the study of American government, we want to create an interdisciplinary process through which it can be studied."

*Teacher A:*  "For example, the subject of American government and its process and implications for the people can be the topic of compositions in the area of writing skills, instruction in reading, a part of the social studies curriculum, and even serve parts of the mathematics area through a study of the budget."

*Supervisor:*  "Have you developed a plan for this work?"

*Teacher A:*  "We have begun to structure our plan. It is not complete, but we thought this meeting with you would help us complete the plan."

*Supervisor:*  "I would be glad to discuss it with you. What do you have so far?"

*Teacher B:*  "Here are our plans. We wish to write a series of model lessons on the subject of the process of American government. These lessons would sequentially develop the major concepts. We should clarify that we intend this study to be of all levels, beginning with local government, then city, state, and finally federal. When all levels have been presented, a special series of lessons will allow the students to compare and contrast the different levels of government."

**Figure 17-3 (continued)**

| | |
|---|---|
| *Teacher A:* | "What's unusual about our idea is that the series of lessons will address as many different subject areas as we can possibly involve. We are sure that the lessons will include language arts, that is, reading and writing; social studies; and mathematics. There may be additional possibilities that will develop." |
| *Teacher B:* | "We would like your approval to implement the model lessons once they are complete to determine how effective the idea is." |
| *Supervisor:* | "Will other members of the faculty be involved?" |
| *Teacher A:* | "Certainly both of us will conduct the model lessons. Would you think it a good idea to open the suggestion to other members of the staff?" |
| *Supervisor:* | "I would certainly support that effort if you wish to do that. It would give you a larger group to judge the effectiveness of the model lessons." |
| *Teacher B:* | "I personally would like to offer the model lessons to interested faculty members if they are willing to give us an evaluation of the effectiveness of the lessons." |
| *Supervisor:* | "If we are in agreement, I will set aside a faculty conference for your presentation of the project and request for participants." |
| *Teacher A:* | "I really think that would be a wonderful idea." |
| *Supervisor:* | "What time frame are you considering?" |
| *Teacher A:* | "I think we need about six weeks to write the model lesson plans. We have all the resources. It is just a matter of organization and time for writing." |
| *Supervisor:* | "I will try to give you some additional time for the project. After the model lessons are completed, how much time will you need to try them with your students?" |
| *Teacher B:* | "We will need about eight weeks to both teach the lessons and have the students complete individual and group projects." |
| *Teacher A:* | "That seems about right. If problems develop, can we ask for an extension of time?" |
| *Supervisor:* | "Certainly. More time will probably be needed for other members of the staff to also try the model lessons. The time frame you have identified appears to be appropriate." |
| *Teacher B:* | "I think the time frame is realistic. We have gathered all of the materials we'll need so we really are all set to go. We also have found a sample curriculum guide that we can use." |
| *Supervisor:* | "Fine. Now, let's discuss the evaluation criteria." |
| *Teacher A:* | "Rather than use tests to evaluate the effectiveness of the model lessons, I would like to use the products that the students create as a result of this course of study." |
| *Supervisor:* | "What type of products are you talking about?" |
| *Teacher B:* | "We plan to ask the students to become involved in creating various individual and group projects based on the teacher-directed lessons that we teach and the research topics that we present to them. These will include reports, original pieces of writing, simulations, brainstorming activities as well as student-designed games, and sample speeches." |

*Teacher A:*    "Those products should be used as the evaluation criteria."

*Supervisor:*    "Student products are the best form of evaluation criteria to judge effectiveness."

*Teacher A:*    "When the course of study has been completed, we could submit the students' products to you and then meet to discuss the products and our experience."

*Supervisor:*    "I am delighted by your supervision plan. I will certainly look forward to seeing the results. Now, let's complete the plan specification form so that we are in agreement about all its aspects."


**Evaluation:**

Student products are submitted within the agreed-upon time frame.

**Plan Evaluation Conference:**

**Objective:**    To discuss the results of the supervision plan.

*Supervisor:*    "How do you feel about the results of your plan?"

*Teacher A:*    "I am personally delighted with the quality of the students' products. They not only created wonderful things, there was also a high level of excitement and interest in the work."

*Teacher B:*    "I also found a high level of student interest in the lessons that were taught. The students were really interested in learning about the process of American government. Some of them are planning to use the government process to solve some school-related problems. Their current idea is to try to get a traffic light at the north side school crossing."

*Teacher A:*    "How did you like the students' products?"

*Supervisor:*    "In general, they were wonderful. All of the students were creatively involved in the subject and there were many superb products created. However, not all the students achieved a high level of understanding of the information. Some of the products, although creative, showed little or no understanding of the topic."

*Teacher B:*    "That is true. The information was difficult and the research materials available were on a difficult reading level. We just did not have enough easy reading material for some of the students. That was a problem we did not deal with."

*Teacher A:*    "How can we deal with the problem?"

*Supervisor:*    "Your plan required tremendous effort and has had such fine results that it really is a shame some students with lower reading levels did not profit to the same degree. Since there really are no materials available on this topic on the lower reading level, the only alternative is to rewrite some of the more difficult materials to make them easier to read. Putting some of the reading materials on tape that the students can listen to would also help."

**Figure 17-3 (continued)**

*Teacher B:*  "That's a wonderful idea. How would such materials be used now that we have completed our plan?"

*Supervisor:*  "Not all the teachers who volunteered to participate have completed the work. They might use the materials if they were available in time. Or, we might offer your interdisciplinary study of American government with the simplified reading materials and tapes to another school. Would that idea be of interest to you?"

*Teacher A:*  "So much work has gone into this supervision plan that I would certainly like to see it made more usable and spread to other schools. I would be willing to continue to work on this curriculum to simplify the research materials."

*Teacher B:*  "I'm in total agreement. The work we have done has had excellent results but we have not provided students with lower reading levels the same opportunities for involvement. I am ready to continue to work."

*Supervisor:*  "The addition of simplified research materials will add tremendously to your curriculum and give it a broader range of use. If we are in agreement, we are ready to complete the plan review and then prepare a new plan specification to match your new objective and plan specifics."

**A New Cycle Has Begun ...**

# Encouraging Self-Directed Supervision

A self-directed supervision plan encourages the individual teacher to supervise his or her efforts for improvement. The success of this plan is dependent upon the ability of the individual teacher to work alone in a constructive and productive manner. As with peer supervision, your confidence in the participating teacher is crucial.

Self-directed supervision is usually the suggestion of the teacher who has a special need or interest. The teacher may have identified a topic or a specific pupil population need. For example, the teacher may be interested in developing a new approach for English second language students. Or, the teacher may be interested in changing a personal style of teaching. For example, the teacher may be interested in developing a literature approach to reading instruction for young children.

In some cases, self-directed supervision may be your suggestion to an individual teacher. You may have identified a grade, department, or school need which is concerned with an area of strength or expertise of a particular teacher. For example, you may wish to involve a teacher, skillful in the teaching of thinking skills, in planning a staff development effort targeted at developing critical-thinking skills in all content areas.

Teachers involved in self-directed supervision determine a supervisory objective. Then, an explicit plan for accomplishing the objective, a time frame for its completion, evaluation criteria for judging the plan's success, and a means of reporting to you are specified. The teacher's plan review report should include a recommendation based on the achieved results. The recommendation may be to terminate the self-directed supervision effort since the objective has been accomplished. If more work on the objective is suggested either by the teacher or you, the supervision plan may be continued.

## HOW TO SELECT THOSE TEACHERS WHO WILL BENEFIT FROM SELF-DIRECTED SUPERVISION

As with peer supervision, the self-directed supervision plan allows the teacher to control and direct his or her supervision plan. The teacher involved must be one of those outstanding professionals who are directed by intrinsic incentives to improve, refine, and create for themselves, their peers, and the profession.

Master teachers may select self-directed supervision for various reasons. Some teachers prefer not to collaborate on creative projects. They find working alone more productive. Others may find self-directed supervision more challenging than peer supervision because they will work in isolation without feedback. Teachers who select self-directed supervision may be motivated by this challenge.

Appropriate candidates for self-directed supervision must be selected with great care. Since the teacher will work alone, there is not even a peer to check on the teacher's progress. The following criteria should be considered:

1. The teacher's analysis and synthesis skills
2. An attitude of respect for and devotion to the teaching profession
3. Whether the teacher is professionally current about ideas, approaches, and materials
4. The teacher's interest in working alone

Teachers who select to work alone should have well-developed analysis skills to properly sort information and explore details. They should be able to design creative and effective solutions that avoid foreseeable pitfalls.

Self-directed supervision is most successful with those teachers who are interested in improving themselves. For these individuals, teaching is more than a job—it is a dedication of the utmost importance. It is the way in which they are able to mold the future.

There must be a source from which to draw when seeking to improve what currently exists. That is why self-directed teachers need to be professionally current about what is being explored in their field. The self-directed teacher must be the kind who seeks out new instructional ideas, approaches, and materials that are discussed in professional journals, papers, and conferences.

Since working alone can often be frustrating and lonely, it should be the teacher's decision. A self-directed supervision plan should not be entered into unless the teacher is sure that it is appropriate for him or her.

## Skill Needs

Self-directed supervision is appropriate for outstanding teachers who seek to refine and improve how the classroom serves pupils. A suggested list of refinement and self-development skills would include those also listed for collaborative and peer supervision. Additional refinement skills include the teacher's ability to:

1. Reorganize existing curriculum
2. Develop alternative curriculum for special student populations
3. Adapt new instructional techniques
4. Implement research implications

## Ability to Analyze and Solve Teaching Problems

Problem identification, analysis, and solution are areas of strength for outstanding or master teachers. In addition, these teachers take the initiative in self-improvement and contributing to the profession without prompting or suggestion. Master teachers, therefore, are particularly suited to making their own selection of a supervisory objective.

## Personal Involvement in Teaching

By definition, master teachers have an extremely high personal involvement in teaching. They feel responsible for both the successes and failures in their classrooms. Since self-directed supervision places such a large degree of responsibility in the hands of the teacher, a high degree of personal involvement is very important to the success of this supervision plan.

Teachers who are appropriate candidates for self-directed supervision show their high degree of personal involvement in teaching in the same ways as do teachers who select peer supervision. Additionally, they demonstrate high involvement by:

1. Exhibiting leadership qualities
2. Enjoying a difficult or challenging task
3. Welcoming change without fear or threat
4. Feeling secure about themselves as teachers at the top of the profession

# THE SELF-DIRECTED SUPERVISION PROCESS

The success of a self-directed supervision plan depends upon the professional attitude of an individual teacher working on an objective of interest and need.

## The Planning Conference

The same objectives should be accomplished in this planning conference as in the planning conference for peer supervision. You should be sure that all five objectives have been accomplished before the conference is concluded. The objectives are restated below:

1. To identify the supervisory objective
2. To outline the plan to be implemented
3. To determine an appropriate time frame
4. To specify evaluation criteria
5. To state that the results of the supervisory effort will be reported to the supervisor

The supervisory objective may come from any source. Usually the objective is identified by an individual teacher. It may come from a need, interest, or new idea that has been suggested by an outside source. Once the teacher has made the decision to work on this particular area, an appointment is made to see you to discuss the objective.

Supervisory objectives may also come from the supervisor who has seen an outstanding practice in one teacher's classroom and wishes to spread that practice. Or, you may have identified a problem that affects various populations within the school. In some cases, you may wish to develop a new approach to a particular population such as mentoring for the gifted.

It is also possible for supervisory objectives to come from other teachers who have identified an important area of need for the school. Or, suggestions may come from parents concerning a school-related problem, such as homework. Supervisory objectives may come from student suggestions or as a result of research reports.

When the idea for a supervisory objective has come from a source other than an individual teacher, you would then look for the appropriate teacher to involve. In this case, the teacher would be invited to a planning conference to discuss the supervisory objective and, if accepted, to plan for its implementation. You must be sure that the teacher understands that the decision to accept or reject the objective rests with him or her. Forcing a teacher to accept a supervisory objective that is not of interest will not produce the desired results.

Once the supervisory objective has been selected, a plan is discussed in detail. (See Figure 18-1.) The teacher who has identified the objective may have also designed an implementation plan. In this case, the plan is reviewed with you. When the teacher has not completed the implementation plan, the planning conference is used to work out the details. Implementation plans for supervisory objectives that come from sources other than the involved teacher are prepared at the planning conference. Teachers who are offered suggested objectives may need time to think through an implementation plan. When this request is made, the planning conference should be postponed.

Your participation in the development of a plan should be limited. A self-directed supervision plan capitalizes on the skills and talents of the professional master teacher. This teacher's creative ideas should be your focus. You should participate only when requested or when you can contribute resources or other types of assistance.

Once the plan has been specified, an appropriate time frame must be selected by the teacher. At best the time frame is an estimate. But the establishment of a time frame sets an expectation for the teacher and gives you a guideline as to when you will see results. The time frame is flexible and may be changed as unforeseen problems occur. When the time frame is changed, you should be notified in writing so the plan specification can be changed.

The evaluation criteria selected should suit the supervisory objective. Usually, the criteria are the results expected from a successful plan implementation. The teacher should select the evaluation criteria from among many alternatives. These evaluation criteria include:

1. Observation of student actions
2. Observation of student products
3. Teacher production of a product
4. Teacher demonstration for other teachers
5. Teacher presentation at workshops or conferences

## The Supervisor's Role

One important role is to help the teacher gain any skill that may be needed to successfully accomplish the supervisory objective. You become the resource for information and materials that support the supervisory effort.

Your second important role is to provide additional time for the teacher to work on the plan. Ths time will be needed to review materials, write drafts, evaluate efforts, and refine the plan. Additional time is especially important if the supervisory objective came from a source other than the involved teacher.

## Monitoring the Involved Teacher

The teacher should be allowed to work on the plan without your intervention. You should not request information unless your participation is requested.

**Figure 18-1**

**Self-Directed Supervision
Plan Specification**

Teacher _____ Class _____ Date _____

**Supervisory Objective:**


**Plan Specifics:**







**Time Frame:**                    **Modification:**


**Evaluation Criteria:**






**The results of the plan will be reported to the supervisor within the time frame.**

Supervisor's Signature _____

Teacher's Signature _____

Your monitoring efforts are better accomplished by encouraging the teacher and reassuring him or her of your continued interest and confidence in the efforts being made. Assess progress informally by asking how things are going. Always make yourself available when solicited.

## The Evaluation

As agreed to in the plan specification, the results should be reported to you within the designated time frame. Any teacher request for modification of the time frame should be made before the due date. You should schedule a plan evaluation conference on the agreed-upon date if the teacher has not done so.

At the evaluation conference, the predetermined evaluation criteria are reviewed and discussed. You and the teacher analyze the results and reach a mutual conclusion about the level of success that has been achieved. The decision to conclude or continue the supervision plan should be agreed upon. When the teacher wishes to continue to work on the plan to further improve it, the original plan specification should be reviewed to determine if it is still appropriate and needs only to have the time frame altered. If the original plan specification is no longer appropriate, it should be modified or rewritten.

# HOW YOU SHOULD REVIEW
# SELF-DIRECTED SUPERVISION

Your written review of self-directed supervision should record what was discussed at the plan review conference. (See Figure 18-2.) Evaluate the supervisory objective as to whether it has been accomplished totally, partially, or not at all. Then review the plan specifics to determine the degree to which they were followed and achieved: successfully, unsuccessfully, or not implemented. Analyze the evaluation criteria and state the degree of their success. The actual time frame used should be recorded. Last, detail whether the decision is to continue the supervision plan, alter the plan specification, or terminate the plan.

# A CASE STUDY OF
# SELF-DIRECTED SUPERVISION

Figure 18-3 is a sample case study that shows self-directed supervision in action. Notes, data, dialogue, and the like, are given.

Figure 18-2

**Self-Directed Supervision
Plan Review**

Teacher _____ Class _____ Date _____

**Supervisory Objective: (accomplished totally / partially / not at all)**

**Plan Specifics: (implemented successfully / unsuccessfully / not implemented)**

**Evaluation Criteria: (high / moderate / low success degree)**

**Time Frame:**

**Future Supervision Plan:**

**Supervisor's Signature** _____

**Teacher's Signature** _____

Figure 18-3

## SELF-DIRECTED SUPERVISION: A CASE STUDY

**Teacher Background:** Fifteen years of successful teaching experience.

**Teacher Type:** High degree of personal involvement in teaching is shown by an excellent attendance record, making herself available for parent conferences both before and after school, involving herself in work related to planning and checking student work both before and after school, being motivated and enthusiastic about teaching, volunteering for work on committees, being respected and admired by her peers, and demonstrating leadership qualities. Has shown a superior degree of the ability to analyze and solve teaching problems by defining actual and potential problems, working to find solution strategies once a problem is identified, being confident in her ability to work with youngsters, and being imaginative and creative.

**Diagnostic Data Used:**

1. Exploration conference
   a. The teacher expressed an interest in redesigning the reading program for her young students.

2. Informal visits
   a. Students are on-task.
   b. Students demonstrate an interest and excitement in learning.
   c. Students self-direct their learning.
   d. Students use the learning environment appropriately within the code of behavior that has been established.

3. Teacher plan review
   a. Plans are detailed and specific concerning the objectives, strategies, and materials to be used.
   b. Plans demonstrate variety and alternatives in the instructional process.

4. Student products review
   a. Student products demonstrate a growth in learning.
   b. Student products are creative and unusual.
   c. Student products illustrate a pride in production.

5. Reported data
   a. The teacher's file is filled with letters of commendation from supervisors, peers, and parents.
   b. Students and parents express confidence in this teacher.

**Supervisory Objective Suggested by the Teacher (refinement need):**

The development of a literature approach to reading instruction for this group of young learners.

**Figure 18-3 (continued)**

**Supervisory Plan Selected:** Self-directed supervision

**Planning Conference:**

**Objective:**    To specify the details of a self-directed supervision plan.

*Supervisor:*    "I have looked forward to this conference. I am interested in hearing what you are thinking about for a supervisory objective."

*Teacher:*    "I am also excited by this project. It is something I have been thinking about for some time, and now I am ready to work on it."

*Supervisor:*    "I know that you usually like to think things through before you discuss them."

*Teacher:*    "That's true. After I have done the thinking, I am ready to share my ideas and hear other points of view."

*Supervisor:*    "If you are ready, tell me what you are thinking about."

*Teacher:*    "I have some very superior readers in my class this year and I want to make reading exciting and meaningful. I think that I can design and implement an ancillary reading program that can run at the same time as the basal."

*Supervisor:*    "Do you mean that you intend to continue with the basal reading program at the same time as you work with the new program?"

*Teacher:*    "That's right. The basal program is basic and contains many important skill development areas. I certainly would not abandon it. But there are other aspects to reading that are not addressed in the basal, skills that relate to higher order analytical skills. I have a group of readers this year who could profit from such instruction."

*Supervisor:*    "What type of skills would you specifically target?"

*Teacher:*    "I am interested in working on character traits and plot identification. I think my students are ready to do this type of analytical work."

*Supervisor:*    "That's very interesting. Have you developed a plan?"

*Teacher:*    "Yes, I have. I am going to start by reading aloud two particular stories that are very different. Each story will be discussed in terms of characters, setting, plot, fact, or fiction. After both stories have been read and discussed, they will be compared for similarities and differences. I plan to continue in this way with a wide variety of stories."

*Supervisor:*    "What do you expect as an outcome?"

*Teacher:*    "I hope that after several group experiences, the children will be able to begin to read and analyze stories on their own. Groups of students can then come together to discuss their reactions."

*Supervisor:*    "What time frame are you considering for this plan?"

*Teacher:*    "I would like to spend at least four weeks reading stories to the group and then discussing and comparing them. I would then like to give the students another four weeks experiencing reading stories themselves and discussing them with other members of the group. I guess about eight weeks would be a good estimate."

*Supervisor:*    "Your time frame seems realistic. Would you like to have some additional planning time if available?"

| | |
|---|---|
| *Teacher:* | "That would be very valuable so I could meet with the librarian to find appropriate books for my presentation and later, for the students' own reading." |
| *Supervisor:* | "Good. What about the evaluation criteria?" |
| *Teacher:* | "I was thinking about inviting you in to see and hear what the students are reading and discussing. I think you will enjoy what I hope will be the development of the ability to analyze literature even at this early stage." |
| *Supervisor:* | "What better evaluation of a plan than to see the students' involvement." |
| *Teacher:* | "After I have invited you to see the students' discussions, I would like to meet with you to discuss the results." |
| *Supervisor:* | "Certainly. I am confident your plan will work well. It is an exciting undertaking. Let's complete the plan specification form so that we are in agreement about all of the details and aspects of the plan." |

## Evaluation:

The supervisor is invited into the classroom to see and hear the students analyze stories they have read independently. This invitation was extended well within the specified time frame.

## Plan Evaluation Conference:

| | |
|---|---|
| **Objective:** | To discuss the results of the evaluation plan. |
| *Supervisor:* | "How do you view the results you have achieved?" |
| *Teacher:* | "I am very pleased about the skills that these students have gained. They really can read, analyze, and discuss those analyses with other students." |
| *Supervisor:* | "I was very impressed with what I saw and heard. The students were capable of discussing their opinions of the story characters. In addition, I was amazed to hear them analyze the plot and identify how the author had planned to carry the story forward. You did an outstanding job. Those youngsters really understand many elements of character traits and plot." |
| *Teacher:* | "Thank you. I, too, am pleased with their progress and mastery of the skills. But there is another element in this skill development that has not yet been approached. I am so encouraged about the results thus far that I would like to suggest a next step." |
| *Supervisor:* | "What do you see as the next step in their development?" |
| *Teacher:* | "I would like to use the students' ability to analyze character traits and story plot in a creative manner. I think the students are now ready to write their own original stories." |
| *Supervisor:* | "That's a wonderful idea. It is the next step in their development and this is certainly the right time to try to develop creative writing skills." |
| *Teacher:* | "I am ready to try a new plan for developing creative writing skills based on the analysis skills they now have." |
| *Supervisor:* | "Well, then, let's complete the plan review and then prepare a new plan specification to meet your new objective and plan specifics." |

**A New Cycle Has Begun ...**

# Understanding the Importance of Your Role As Supervisor

Change is almost always difficult, but change without explanation and clarification is traumatic. Before you attempt to implement a program of individualized supervision plans, matched to diagnosed teacher needs, take the time to introduce and discuss the overall program with your staff. Explain what an individualized supervision plan is, how it will work, and how it will be of value to them. Involve the teachers by providing the opportunity for them to express their feelings and explore their concerns. Then, motivate and encourage teacher efforts throughout the individualized supervision process by being generous with your time, resources, and instructional support.

## HOW TO INTRODUCE INDIVIDUALIZED SUPERVISION PLANS TO THE FACULTY

Supervision plans are most successfully implemented when they are both understood and accepted by the staff. Teachers must clearly understand how the individualized plan will impact on them. They must believe that the supervision plan will help rather than harm them. Their trust and confidence in you, as supervisor, based on past experience, will contribute to their acceptance of your new supervision program. But, their final acceptance will come only after they have actually experienced the supervision effort and discovered that not only were they not harmed but, rather, they were supported and helped.

## Where and When to Present the Plans

Gaining staff understanding and acceptance of a supervisory program based on individualized supervision plans begins with a full faculty introduction. The meeting used to present the rationale and concepts behind such plans should be carefully thought out. If possible, present your ideas at a time when no other matter of urgent need must be discussed. Individualized supervision plans, based on needs, should be the only important item on the agenda.

Faculty conferences may be used for this purpose. Since all members of the faculty will be present, this conference provides the opportunity to address the total faculty at the same time. This gives you the advantage of a uniform presentation. In addition, the entire faculty will benefit from hearing the ideas, concerns, and questions expressed by their peers at this meeting.

Too often, however, large group presentations can discourage open discussion. This disadvantage may be overcome by presenting the topic a second time during grade or department meetings. The security of a smaller group will encourage some teachers to express their feelings, fears, and questions. This second presentation will also provide another opportunity for teachers to become familiar with individualized supervision plans.

When teacher concern and acceptance are a problem, the topic may be addressed at workshop sessions before or after school hours, during the lunch hour, or during staff development programs. These additional sessions may be important to clarify the process and its implications for the individual teacher.

## What to Explain

Target your explanation at promoting the understanding that rather than lump all teachers into the same category, in which they are all treated the same, individualized plans recognize the skill level of individual teachers. The following clarifications should be made at the presentation sessions:

1. **The plans are individualized.** Teacher supervision needs are differentiated. Those who need specific guided assistance can count on personalized assistance. Other teachers who require little or no help will be provided with the opportunity to design and direct their efforts in areas in which they are interested.

**2. The plans seek to be meaningful and effective.** Teachers are treated as individuals. Each teacher is involved in working on objectives that represent skill needs expressed by the individual teacher and/or the supervisor.

**3. The plans respect the professional skills of teachers.** The plans are designed to recognize the successful accomplishment levels of experienced teachers. Various diagnostic techniques are used to confirm teaching skills that have been mastered and to identify areas of need.

**4. The plans provide for involvement of teachers in the selection of objective and type of supervision plan.** The plans provide for a wide range of involvement by the professional staff, from total control of the objective and plan selection (as in peer and self-directed supervision), to limited selection of objective and plan (as in collaborative supervision), to directed selection of objective and supervision plan (as in intensive guided supervision). This variety results in a plan appropriate for the needs and interests of each teacher.

## MAXIMIZING THE BENEFITS OF EACH SUPERVISION PLAN

An individualized and diversified supervision plan based on the diagnosed needs of each teacher saves you time and makes best use of your efforts. As the needs of the individual teacher are clarified and the plan is selected and implemented, your level and degree of involvement become clear. You then know how much of your time and effort will be required to make the supervision effort effective and can, therefore, allocate your time efficiently and effectively.

### Make Time Your Ally

You can control the number of intensive guided supervision plans you wish to be involved with at any given time. From this, you can judge how much time you will have to be involved with collaborative supervision plans. You will also know how many peer and self-directed plans you will be able to initiate. In this way, time for your supervisory efforts with the entire staff can be realistically allocated. You will find it easier to apportion time for the completion of other administrative efforts.

### Motivate Teachers Through Trust

An individualized supervision plan utilizes time effectively because it motivates teachers to action. Teachers' accomplishments are recognized and, therefore, their self-confidence is developed. This confidence will inspire them to continue to seek growth. Success and recognition lead to greater success and increased recognition.

It is therefore a good idea to place your trust in the teacher when in doubt about a supervision plan. The teacher's enthusiasm is most important. Taking a chance on a less-directed supervision plan will encourage the teacher to succeed.

Keep the momentum going through praise and recognition. Each teacher's efforts should be recognized and rewarded. A letter from you and/or a public announcement of efforts can result in tangible rewards of further accomplishments. The greatest result of your recognition efforts will be the motiviation of the teachers to strive even harder.

## THE SUPERVISOR AS TEACHER

You are the principal teacher in the school. Your background and experience provide valuable direction for teachers' efforts.

### Giving In-Class Instructional Support

You provide the teacher with a valuable model to copy when you actually teach a lesson or participate in the development of a plan. One demonstration is worth ten thousand words. Do not hesitate to go into the classroom to show the teacher exactly what you want that teacher to do.

Admittedly, you are at a disadvantage. You do not know the students and you may not be familiar with the topic. However, you can select a different topic, one suited to your area of expertise, for the demonstration. Your position as supervisor will easily overcome any difficulties that might be anticipated by your lack of knowledge of the students. If you are concerned about not knowing the youngsters' names, ask the teacher to have each student prepare a visible name card before you enter the classroom.

In-class coaching is a second effective model. The one model lesson may not be sufficient to instruct the teacher in the desired actions. Spending time in the classroom as a coach, helping the teacher thoroughly understand the technique or strategy, may be very effective. If you cannot spend the time needed, or if you do not think you have the specific skills required, arrange to provide a coach who does have the time and the skills. Coaches may be found among other teachers on the staff or among district office personnel.

A teacher "buddy" support system is a third effective in-class support system. Peer teachers in the school may work in pairs to demonstrate specific areas of expertise for each other. This colleague-to-colleague assistance is a most effective way to help teachers learn instructional strategies. This system may be part of a peer supervision plan, or it may be an addition to any other supervision plan.

## Giving Out-of-Class Instructional Support

Many out-of-class instructional support efforts suffer from the "too much, too fast" effect. These efforts provide only for teacher exposure to the idea, practice, or strategy. Exposure is very different from effective application, which requires guided practice and feedback to the teacher. That is why all out-of-class instructional support efforts should provide classroom application if they are to be successful.

In-service training, intended to provide information about new programs and practices, is a popular out-of-class instructional support system used widely throughout the country. Although many of these in-service efforts are well intended and even well-designed, they often fail. Teachers cannot be expected to understand, digest, and implement new ideas or strategies after one or even two or three large group presentations. Better results are generally achieved when the teachers are given time to experience and then react to the strategies.

University work is usually a good means of providing out-of-class instructional support when the material presented is practical and if the professor also provides a means for the teachers to try the practices discussed and present their experiences. Actual in-class application is necessary to ensure the teacher's appropriate application of the strategy or technique.

Professional publications are a good source of out-of-class instructional support. This is especially true when what is written is explicit and applicable to the teacher's class experience. The effectiveness of journals and other professional publications is directly related to the teacher's interest in the topic.

# OBTAINING TEACHER EVALUATION OF YOUR SUPERVISORY EFFORTS

Everybody needs feedback to truly evaluate effectiveness. Supervisors are no exception. Do you want to know how your staff views you and your involvement with them? Then ask them to rate you. If you are serious about your efforts and impact, these ratings will provide valuable information.

## Evaluation Criteria

The supervisor's position is more than a job, a role, a profession—it is a total involvement in the lives, feelings, actions, and efforts of the school population. Being a supervisor is a "people position."

A supervisor is a:

1. Resource and a source for resources

2. Guide who leads, directs, and suggests

3. Comrade who shares success, failure, joy, and despair

4. Dreamer of what could be, should be, and will be

That is why it is so very difficult to reduce the role of supervisor to a list of items. However, Figure 19-1 presents a suggested list of items by which you may be rated. It is an attempt to capture most of the items that are important. The items are grouped into three categories: your attitude toward teachers, how to motivate teacher efforts, and your leadership skills.

**Your Attitude Toward Teachers.** This category concerns itself with what you think about teachers and how you treat them. Characteristics of a positive attitude toward teachers include listening to as well as soliciting and respecting teachers' opinions, suggestions, and concerns. Another aspect of a positive attitude is being open-minded, honest, and sensitive in your daily dealings with teachers.

**How You Motivate Teachers.** This second category deals with how you get things done. The items listed are positive motivators rather than heavy-handed demands. Techniques used by a motivator include encouraging, inspiring, and stimulating teacher efforts and initiative. The motivator demonstrates creative and friendly behavior in his or her work with teachers.

**Leadership Skills.** The last category targets the ways in which you lead, guide, and direct the school staff. These leadership characteristics deal with your skill in providing resources, suggestions, and constructive criticism. Taking the responsibility for leadership is demonstrated by accepting obligation, facing conflicts, and handling problems.

## Using the Supervisor's Rating Form

Introduce the form to the teachers with a sincere request for their honest and open feedback. Clarify that you really want to know what they think and how they feel about you. If you want teachers to be honest and open, ask them not to identify themselves. Remaining anonymous prevents distortion of responses because of fear of reprisal or desire to curry favor. Responses that are not honest are of no value.

The teachers are asked to rate you on each item using a scale from 4 to 0. You may wish to take a few moments to explain the scale:

4 – Always (evidence is apparent *at all times*)

3 – Most of the time (evidence is *usually* apparent)

2 – Some of the time (evidence is apparent *once in a while*)

1 – Rarely (evidence is *usually not* apparent)

0 – Never (evidence is *never* apparent)

Figure 19-1

| THE SUPERVISOR'S RATING FORM | | 4 | 3 | 2 | 1 | 0 |
|---|---|---|---|---|---|---|
| ATTITUDE TOWARD TEACHERS | listens to teachers | | | | | |
| | solicits teachers' opinions | | | | | |
| | solicits teachers' suggestions | | | | | |
| | respects teachers' opinions | | | | | |
| | is open-minded | | | | | |
| | considers feelings | | | | | |
| | respects teachers' concerns | | | | | |
| | is honest | | | | | |
| MOTIVATOR OF TEACHERS | encourages teachers' efforts | | | | | |
| | encourages teachers' initiative | | | | | |
| | is inspiring | | | | | |
| | is creative | | | | | |
| | is stimulating | | | | | |
| | is friendly | | | | | |
| LEADERSHIP SKILLS | gives valuable suggestions | | | | | |
| | criticizes constructively | | | | | |
| | provides resources | | | | | |
| | faces conflicts | | | | | |
| | handles problems | | | | | |
| | accepts responsibilities | | | | | |

Please rate your supervisor for each item above. Place an X under the selected number using the following scale.

4 – ALWAYS (evidence is apparent at all times)

3 – MOST OF THE TIME (evidence is usually apparent)

2 – SOME OF THE TIME (evidence is apparent once in a while)

1 – RARELY (evidence is usually not apparent)

0 – NEVER (evidence is never apparent)

This form should be returned to the supervisor's letter box WITHOUT YOUR SIGNATURE. Thank you for your honest response.

## Analyzing the Results

Hopefully, every member of the teaching staff will return the form to the place you have designated. Post a reminder notice if you do not receive all the completed forms within a week.

There are several ways to analyze the results. The chart below lists the total number of items and the highest possible score for each category and the total rating form:

| Category | Number of Items | Highest Possible Score |
|----------|-----------------|------------------------|
| Attitude | 8 | 32 |
| Motivator | 6 | 24 |
| Leadership | 6 | 24 |
| Total | 20 | 80 |

1. Calculate your total scores. Compare each form's total score with the highest possible score. Add all the scores together and divide by the total number of forms that were returned. That figure is your average. Find your lowest and highest score to determine the range of scores you received.

2. Calculate your category scores. Compare your scores with the highest possible scores for each category. Add all the category scores together and divide by the total number of forms that were returned. That figure is your average. Find your lowest and highest scores in each category to determine the range of scores you received.

3. Do a score comparison. This information helps to give you a summary view of the staff's evaluation of you.

## How to Do a Score Comparison for Total Scores

List the numbers 0 to 80 in a column. Count and record the number of forms that totaled each score. For example, the number of forms that totaled 80, 65, 24, and so forth. Now consider the score range. Figure 19-2 shows how to calculate and interpret the scores.

Think about the score range of 0 to 80 in four parts. Specifically:

  0 to 20 = the lowest fourth
21 to 40 = the second fourth
41 to 60 = the third fourth
61 to 80 = the highest fourth

Group the number of scores in each fourth. Now, calculate the percentage of responses for each fourth by dividing the number of response forms in each fourth by the total

**Figure 19-2**

### Total Score Comparison

| Score | Number of Forms | Range Group |
|-------|-----------------|-------------|
| 80 | 2 | |
| 75 | 5 | |
| 68 | 3 | 14 |
| 65 | 2 | |
| 63 | 2 | |
| 57 | 1 | |
| 45 | 1 | 3 |
| 41 | 1 | |
| 33 | 1 | 2 |
| 25 | 1 | |
| 18 | 1 | 1 |
| Total Forms | 20 | 20 |

number of possible response forms. For example, 14 responses divided by a total of 20 response forms equals 70 percent. In Figure 19-2:

- 14 forms or 70 percent of the staff rated this supervisor above 60.
- 3 forms or 15 percent of the staff rated this supervisor between 41 and 60.
- 2 forms or 10 percent of the staff rated this supervisor between 21 and 40.
- 1 form or 5 percent of the staff rated this supervisor between 0 and 20.
- Overall, 85 percent of the staff rated this supervisor above 40 out of a possible score of 80.

## How to Do a Score Comparison for Category Scores

A score comparison may be done in the same way for each category. List the numbers 0 to 32 for the attitude category and 0 to 24 for the motivator and leadership categories. Count and record the number of forms that totaled the same category score. Figure 19-3 shows how to calculate and interpret the category scores.

## Figure 19-3

### Attitude Category Score Comparison

| Score | Number of Forms | Range Group |
|-------|-----------------|-------------|
| 32 | 2 | |
| 30 | 2 | 8 |
| 26 | 4 | |
| 20 | 5 | 10 |
| 18 | 5 | |
| 13 | 1 | 2 |
| 9 | 1 | |
| **Total Forms** | **20** | **20** |

Think about the score range of 0 to 32 in four parts.

Specifically:  0 to 8 = the lowest fourth
9 to 16 = the second fourth
17 to 24 = the third fourth
25 to 32 = the highest fourth

Group the number of scores in each fourth. Now, calculate the percentage of responses for each fourth by dividing the number of response forms in each fourth by the total number of possible response forms. For example, 8 responses divided by a total of 20 response forms equals 40 percent. In Figure 19-3:

- 8 forms or 40 percent of the staff rated this supervisor above 24.
- 10 forms or 50 percent of the staff rated this supervisor between 17 and 24.
- 2 forms or 10 percent of the staff rated this supervisor between 9 and 16.
- 0 forms or 0 percent of the staff rated this supervisor between 0 and 8.
- Overall, 90 percent of the staff rated this supervisor above 16 out of a possible score of 32.

For the categories of motivator and leadership, think about the score range of 0 to 24 in four parts.

Specifically:   0 to 6 = the lowest fourth
7 to 12 = the second fourth
13 to 18 = the third fourth
19 to 24 = the highest fourth

Group the number of scores in each fourth. Now, calculate the percentage of responses for each fourth in the same way, by dividing the number of response forms in each fourth by the total number of possible response forms.

## USING THE RESULTS OF THE EVALUATION

You may be surprised, delighted, disappointed, or in disagreement with the results. Remember, the scores represent the staff's point of view. Now you know your instructional staff's overall view of you as a supervisor as well as their categorical rating of your attitude toward them, your motivational efforts, and your leadership abilities. Using the results as a guide in the future will increase your effectiveness.

Reflect honestly on the category and items that have low ratings. Itemize specific examples of your actions or behavior that may have resulted in that rating. You may choose to add to these examples by consulting with selected staff members with whom you have an open relationship. Ask them to contribute their ideas to the list of examples you have itemized.

Now that you have a good source of data, use it to change your actions and behavior. Match each example of a low-rated behavior or action with several positive alternatives to that action.

For example, if you were rated low in the attitude category on the item, "listens to teachers," try these alternatives when a teacher wishes to talk with you:

1. Stop and take the time to listen.

2. Tell the teacher you will join him or her for coffee during the lunch hour.

3. Make a mutually convenient appointment and keep it.

As another example, if you were rated low in the motivator category on the item, "is friendly," try these alternatives:

1. Be aware of your body language.

2. Smile even when you don't feel like it.

3. Ask about the health and welfare of the family of individual staff members.

4. Make occasional positive comments about staff appearance.

As a last example, if you were rated low in the leadership category on the item, "criticizes constructively," try these alternatives:

1. Always begin with a positive comment.
2. Offer reasons for the occurrence of the criticized actions.
3. Concentrate on suggestions for improvement rather than dwell on the criticism.
4. Graciously accept a teacher's apology, suggestion, promise, or the like.

In your daily interactions, remember your commitment to raise your rating. Before taking an action or reacting to a situation, consider some of the alternatives. The most effective supervisor is one who is viewed positively by the staff in attitude, motivation, and leadership.

## THE SUPERVISOR AS AN INDIVIDUAL OR AS A MEMBER OF A TEAM

This book may be used as effectively in settings where one or more assistants form a supervisory team as it is in settings where there is only one supervisor.

For the supervisor who is alone, this book provides the specific strategies, techniques, and details needed to tailor supervision so that it is both effective and efficient.

In settings where there is more than one supervisor, using this book for a team approach will reap rewards. The approach of tailoring supervision to teacher needs is the same in this case as when there is a lone supervisor. The difference in using a team approach is in the number of supervisory plans for which each supervisor will be responsible.

The supervisory team should detail a specific strategy for assigning supervisory responsibilities. Various strategies will work equally well. The selection of one rather than another will depend upon the specific staff needs of each setting.

## WHY SHOULD YOU ASSIGN PARTICULAR SUPERVISION RESPONSIBILITIES TO OTHERS?

There are several different ways in which you can and should assign responsibilities to other supervisors. These, and the rationale for each, include:

1. Each supervisor will assume responsibility for some of the new teachers. *Rationale:* There are a large number of new teachers in the school, each of whom would benefit from intensive guided supervision. Since this form of supervision is the most time-consuming, the load should logically be shared.

2. One supervisor will work with all the new teachers. *Rationale:* There are only a few new teachers on the staff who will benefit from intensive guided supervision. One supervisor may become an expert in this form of supervision.

3. Each supervisor will assume supervision responsibility for some marginal teachers. *Rationale:* There are a large number of marginal teachers on the staff, each of whom would profit from intensive guided supervision. This type of supervisory assignment can be frustrating and should be equally shared.

4. One supervisor will assume supervision responsibility for all the marginal teachers. *Rationale:* There are only a few marginal teachers on the staff who require intensive guided supervision. One supervisor may be interested in this challenge.

5. Each supervisor will be assigned supervisory responsibility for a specific age/grade level. *Rationale:* The school staff is equally represented with new, marginal, and experienced teachers on all age/grade levels. An individual supervisor may be more experienced and comfortable with a particular age/grade level.

## MEETING WITH THE SUPERVISION TEAM

The supervision team should meet from time to time to share their experiences. Three benefits result from the team's sharing of their supervisory work:

1. The specific supervisory plans for each teacher are explained and discussed, providing a supervision overview for the school.

2. Effective strategies and techniques are shared, expanding their use to other supervisors.

3. The supervisory team may serve as a resource to brainstorm solutions to trouble spots that some supervisors may be experiencing.

In this way, the supervisory team may be maximally effective, both individually and collectively, as contributors to the overall supervisory process.

# How to Communicate Successfully

# Establishing a Secure Climate

Your primary goal is the achievement of a maximally functioning school filled with happy, efficient, and effective teachers. Establishing a standard for excellence in teaching (discussed in Part I), knowing teacher needs (discussed in Part II), and matching supervision to those needs (discussed in Part III), are important elements in making teachers efficient and effective. But what are the elements that will achieve your goal of making teachers happy? This subject now deserves study.

Being happy is a function of attitude and perception: the more positive the attitude and perception, the happier the individual and, generally, the more successful the performance. This section explains how to establish a secure climate so that teachers will develop the positive attitudes and perceptions that generate successful teaching performance.

## THE IMPACT OF BASIC HUMAN NEEDS ON TEACHERS' ROLES

**193**

The importance and significance of basic human needs cannot be escaped. These needs are usually classified in a hierarchy that ranges from the uncomplicated physical to the complex psychological. Each need impacts on how teachers function, act, react, and therefore, perform their role as instructors of students.

## Physical Needs

Because they are essential for survival, the physical needs are the most powerful of all. They include the need for food, water, air, shelter, and sleep. The lack of satisfaction of any one of these physical needs will totally prevent the individual from functioning. No other concern can be attended to until these needs are met. Yet, the abuse of these needs may become the means by which people express unmet higher order needs—we all know people who overeat or suffer from insomnia.

Be alert to these indicators of unmet needs among your staff. Although needs involved with the personal life of staff members are beyond your control, your understanding, sensitivity, and sympathy will help the individual function better. On the other hand, those unmet needs may relate to school problems over which you do have control. Each of the basic needs is discussed in terms of its relationship to school life.

## The Need to Be Safe

When physical needs are satisfied at an adequate level, the next need level, safety, demands satisfaction. Feeling safe involves the need to live in a world that is predictable and consistent to some degree. This provides the individual with a realistic expectation of what to do, how to do it, and what the outcomes will be. Although it is true that change is inevitable and crisis must be faced, they do not have to be faced on a daily basis.

People with unmet safety needs appear anxious and insecure. Not only do they stop taking risks, they become defensive, even neurotic. This behavior is easily recognized in children who have been removed from their home and family.

Teachers with an unmet need to be safe exhibit the following behavior. They avoid any change. This may include a refusal to:

1. Use new materials
2. Implement a new program
3. Rearrange the classroom furniture
4. Change their program or duty
5. Change their seat in the lunchroom

In addition, these teachers may become negative, critical, and defensive. This may be shown by their need to:

1. Justify their actions
2. Criticize other staff members, students, and materials
3. Find fault with everything around them
4. Act suspicious about the intent of decisions that involve them

Teachers new to the school may feel unsafe in an unknown situation. When they do, they are nervous and fearful. They may appear to be distant and aloof preferring isolation to interaction.

You can help teachers satisfy the need to feel safe by:

- Establishing rules that are observed consistently. For example, consistently do not allow teachers to carry hot coffee through the halls.

- Specifying a realistic expectation for teacher performance of administrative and instructional tasks. For example, collect plans on the specified day or require all teachers to teach reading every day.

- Maintaining consistent procedures for dealing with routine matters. For example, books are always ordered by completing a specific form and placing it in a particular box.

- Meeting teacher expectations for commendation and confrontation. For example, commend teacher efforts by writing a letter, or confront teachers by calling them to a conference.

## The Need to Belong

Following the satisfaction of the need to be safe, the next higher need, to belong, will motivate individuals. This is the need to be understood, accepted, and liked by persons and the organization in our daily lives. We all strive with intensity to satisfy this need.

When the need to belong is thwarted and unsatisfied, the individual will restrict or abort efforts, energy, and commitment. Since everyone strives to achieve a sense of belonging, that energy, effort, and commitment will be directed at new potential targets.

Teachers whose need to belong is unmet by the school organization and its staff will withdraw from the school community by:

1. Isolating themselves from others
2. Eating alone
3. Not attending group social functions
4. Not contributing to group work sessions
5. Avoiding the faculty lounge

Teachers sometimes inappropriately look to their students to satisfy the need to belong and be valued. To accomplish this they:

1. Select pet students
2. Buy student affection with favors
3. Apply class rules inconsistently to favor particular youngsters
4. Attempt to make students dependent upon them

Other students not targeted for satisfaction of the need may:

1. Become angry at unfair treatment
2. Be threatened by what they perceive as injustice
3. Begin to dislike the teacher
4. Form supportive defense groups
5. Verbally attack the teacher
6. Complain to their parents who bring the matter to your attention

Teachers can be supported in their need to belong, to be liked, and accepted by your:

- Warmth and friendliness. For example, a morning smile, an afternoon wish for a pleasant evening, a question about the health and well-being of the person and his or her family.
- Encouragement of colleague work groups. For example, by giving the work groups time to meet, by encouraging and being accepting of their efforts.
- Approval of social gatherings. For example, by assisting efforts to plan such events.
- Active participation in socializing efforts for new and isolated staff members. For example, by contributing to and attending staff social functions.
- Efforts to resolve interpersonal conflicts. For example, holding a meeting targeted at resolution of the differences and involving other staff members who may be of help.
- Attention to the need to provide comfortable and attractive meeting places. For example, assisting staff efforts to paint and decorate staff rooms.

## The Need for Esteem

When the need to belong and be accepted is satisfied, the next higher need, personal esteem, will be felt. This need drives us to seek approval and respect from others. When this need is met, we feel confident about our ability and competence to act effectively. Our achievements have been acknowledged and respected, making us sure of our performance.

The satisfaction of the need for esteem is inhibited in school organizations that do not provide the means to recognize, acknowledge, and prize staff achievements. The results of this inhibiting behavior cause teachers to:

1. Feel threatened
2. Feel insecure about their efforts
3. Mistrust you and the school organization
4. Be discouraged
5. Not take initiative and responsibility

Teachers can be helped to fulfill the need for esteem by your:

- Public recognition of their efforts. For example, a letter of commendation placed in the teacher's file and the parents' association bulletin, if appropriate.
- Valuing their achievement. For example, asking them to be speakers at faculty conferences.
- Respecting their status. For example, asking the teacher's permission before removing a student from the class.

## ACTIONS AND ATTITUDES THAT FOSTER SECURITY

Staff members use various indicators to judge the security of the school climate. Many of these indicators relate to the staff's perception of you. Both your actions toward them and your attitude in dealing with them will be interpreted as indicators of a secure or insecure climate. The behaviors which follow foster security and therefore encourage staff performance.

### Being Honest

Communicate in an open and honest manner. Make honest statements about your feelings, attitudes, and reactions to situations. Be honest even when it is easier not to tell the truth. Once discovered in an untruth, your honesty will never again be trusted. For example, Ms. X was given the new set of texts. Ms. Y wants to know why she did not get them. An honest answer might involve a discussion of how Ms. Y's former classes have abused materials. It is important to remember, however, that honesty is always tempered with tact.

### Being Tactful

Be sensitive to staff needs, feelings, and problems. Treat them in a nonthreatening manner. For example, be tactful when discussing why the new texts were not placed in Ms. Y's class. Do not label Ms. Y's classroom or her appearance. You are nonthreatening when you avoid telling Ms. Y that she will not get new materials until she demonstrates neatness and demands it of her class.

## Accepting People As They Are

Respect people's individual differences, opinions, perceptions, and approaches. This individuality offers variety to the school. In addition, there is no one way to do anything. For example, Ms. Z tells you she does not wish to use the new film to introduce the unit on colonial America. She says that the film has a sex bias. She offers an alternative introduction. You show acceptance of her opinion and perception when you agree to her plan.

## Having a Positive Approach

Project yourself as a warm, likeable person who is concerned about everyone. This encouraging behavior and attitude leads people to believe they are important, valued, and supported. You demonstrate a positive approach when you greet people, smile at them, and inquire about their health, problems, and constraints. Your first reaction to a problem should be nonjudgmental, showing faith in the staff member. For example, a positive approach to Ms. Y's problem of class abuse of materials might be to promise her the next new set of suitable texts. This may lead her to believe that she does have the ability to change and that you have faith in that ability.

## Being Dependable

When you are dependable, you are trusted. What you promise is believed because you keep your word. When circumstances prevent you from keeping your word, tell the involved person about it as soon as possible. For example, when a new set of suitable texts arrive, keep your promise to Ms. Y, and send them to her. Chances are that your positive approach and dependability will encourage her to be sure that the texts receive good treatment. Just think about how she will feel and behave if she finds out you gave the next new set of texts to another teacher. By that action you will have told her that you do not believe she can change and that your word should not be trusted.

# THE IMPORTANCE OF NONVERBAL COMMUNICATION

All of us communicate without speech or print. Our nonverbal language sends powerful messages to everyone around us. Consider the following incident: A smiling teacher enters the supervisor's office for a conference. She stops smiling as soon as she sees the supervisor and sinks into a chair. Although the supervisor has not said or written anything, a message has been sent and received.

Nonverbal language is a powerful tool that should not be used unconsciously. When it is used without thought and purpose, opportunities to motivate, encourage, and support desired actions may be lost. Or, resulting negative reactions may prevent you from reaching your goals.

Positive use of nonverbal communication is achieved in two ways:

1. By practicing positive nonverbal communication.
2. By being aware of negative nonverbal communication when it is practiced by yourself and others.

## Positive Nonverbal Communication

The visible actions of positive nonverbal communication send the following messages:

1. Your total attention is focused on the other person.
2. You are interested in the other person.
3. You are sensitive to the other person's needs and concerns.
4. You are involved with the other person.

You are practicing positive nonverbal communication with your body, arms, hands, face, and voice when you do the following:

- *Body*—Sit next to or across from the other person. Relax your body and turn to face the other person. Lean forward toward the other person. Move slowly and infrequently during the meeting.
- *Arms*—Keep your arms relaxed and open, resting on the table, the arm of the chair, or in your lap.
- *Hands*—Keep your hands open with the palms facing up. Use your hands to gesture or to lightly touch the other person.
- *Face*—Show expression on your face. Smile frequently. Look directly at the other person with open eyes.
- *Voice*—Use a calm, cordial, and expressive voice and fluid speech.

## Negative Nonverbal Communication

The visible actions of negative nonverbal communication send the following messages. You or the other person is:

1. Distracted or disinterested
2. Suspicious and on guard against harm

**Figure 20-1**

## NONVERBAL COMMUNICATION

| | POSITIVE | NEGATIVE |
|---|---|---|
| **Body** | sit next to the person | sit behind a desk |
| | body relaxed | body tense |
| | body turned to face | body turned away |
| | lean toward | lean away |
| | move slowly | move quickly |
| | move infrequently | move frequently |
| **Arms** | relaxed | tense |
| | open | crossed |
| **Hands** | palms up | hands clenched/fingers intertwined |
| | use to gesture | do not use |
| | touch other person lightly | point with finger |
| **Face** | expressive | frozen |
| | smiling | frowning/deadpan look |
| | look at person | look elsewhere |
| | eyes open | eyes blink often |
| **Voice** | calm | high-pitched |
| | expressive | inaudible |
| | speech fluid | speech hesitant |

3. Nervous and fearful about the outcome

4. Angry and hostile

You or others are practicing negative nonverbal communication with the body, arms, hands, face, and voice when you or they do the following:

- *Body*—Sit at a desk with the other person at the side of the desk or in front of the desk, placing an authoritarian barrier between the persons. Tense the body and turn away from the other person. Lean back, away from the other person. Move quickly and frequently during the meeting.

- *Arms*—Keep the arms tense and crossed or out of sight.

- *Hands*—Close or clench the hands or intertwine the fingers. Do not use the hands except for finger pointing.

- *Face*—Present a "frozen" facial expression, showing only a frown or a "deadpan" look. Focus the eyes elsewhere, not directly on the other person, and blink frequently.

- *Voice*—Use a high, almost inaudible, voice and hesitant speech.

Figure 20-1 presents a comparative summary of positive and negative nonverbal communication.

When you practice positive nonverbal communication you place the other person or persons at ease. Your behavior and attitude make them feel secure, valued, and comfortable. You create the atmosphere that gives you a maximum opportunity to accomplish your goals.

When you recognize that someone else is using negative nonverbal communication in your presence, do not reciprocate by practicing the same actions. They will only inhibit you from reaching your goals. As you study the other person you will recognize the fear, suspicion, and anger he or she demonstrates. Now you have the opportunity to use positive verbal and nonverbal communication to calm that person and make him or her feel safe so that mutual goals can be achieved.

# Conducting Successful Conferences

The conference is the supervisor's most powerful tool. It provides the opportunity to talk with the teacher and accomplish two specific objectives:

1. To transmit effective feedback to the teacher about what he or she is doing.

2. To use that feedback to form an action plan aimed at improving teacher performance.

## GUIDELINES FOR TRANSMITTING FEEDBACK

The success of the conference is dependent upon how the supervisor transmits feedback to the teacher. Feedback that is transmitted in *effective* ways:

1. Develops a helping teacher-supervisor relationship

2. Is accepted by the teacher

3. Provides the groundwork for an improvement plan

Feedback that is transmitted in *ineffective* ways:

1. Develops an adversary teacher-supervisor relationship
2. Is rejected by the teacher
3. Hinders the development of an improvement plan

## Effective Feedback Is Objective, While Ineffective Feedback Is Subjective

### Observation vs. Assumption

• Objective feedback focuses on what was actually observed rather than on making an assumption about what happened. It is possible to observe the teacher call consistently on the same three or four youngsters. To state that the teacher involved only three or four youngsters in the lesson is an assumption. The teacher should have the opportunity to discuss why he or she took this action.

• It is possible to observe that the students had difficulty seeing the small picture that the teacher held up during the lesson. It is an assumption to state that the teacher was too lazy to find more suitable material. The observation statement is useful in helping teachers think about better ways to demonstrate and illustrate concepts. The assumption statement puts teachers on the defensive and encourages them to justify their actions.

### Description vs. Evaluation

• Objective feedback describes what took place rather than evaluates how good or bad it was. It is better to describe the difficulty that most of the students had in completing the follow-up sheet than to evaluate the lesson with the statement that the children learned nothing. Describing the difficulty the children had leads the teacher to talk about why that happened. Evaluating that the children learned nothing encourages the teacher to defend the lesson.

• You can describe the poor behavior of several children in the back of the room and involve the teacher in finding reasons for this. If instead, you give an evaluation of poor classroom management, the teacher will tell you all the management techniques he or she used that were effective.

## Effective Feedback Is Realistic, While Ineffective Feedback Is Idealistic

### Concrete vs. Abstract

• Realistic feedback deals with concrete specifics rather than global abstractions. It is far more understandable to tell a teacher about a useful filmstrip available from the media center than to tell that teacher to make the lesson more interesting.

• When discipline is an important topic in the conference, a discussion of behavior management techniques is a concrete solution that the teacher may be able to try. To tell the teacher that he or she must have better control of the youngsters will probably not help the situation.

### Manageable vs. Impossible

• Realistic feedback deals with a manageable number of areas to work on at one time. Trying to work on everything at once causes an impossible overload and results in nothing being accomplished. Involve the teacher in the selection of areas to work on. If you have supervisory priorities, state them, giving the reasons for their selection, and involve the teacher in an understanding and agreement.

• Some areas interact and may be sensible and practical to work on at the same time. For example, developing critical-thinking questions that require student reaction and discussion will lead to increased student involvement in the lesson. This usually prevents the teacher from dominating the lesson. Therefore, it may be possible to work on questioning techniques, student involvement, and teacher dominance at the same time.

### Changeable vs. Fixed

• Realistic feedback focuses on what is changeable rather than wastes time on what is fixed and cannot be changed. It is possible to help a teacher better plan a time frame in which to complete a specific unit of work. Complaining over lost time because the teacher took six weeks instead of three weeks to cover the last unit will not help.

• It is more productive to work with the teacher on how to help the students keep their work in good order using the notebooks they have, than to spend time talking about how much better looseleaf books would have been.

### Current vs. Past

• Realistic feedback deals with accurate memory of events. Conferences should be scheduled as soon as possible after an observation so that the information is fresh in the minds of both the teacher and the supervisor. Memories of events that happened in the past are often vague and sometimes inaccurate.

## Effective Feedback Is Motivating, While Ineffective Feedback Is Demanding

### Giving Information vs. Giving Advice

• Motivating feedback provides information and encourages the teacher to participate in the discussion of the event. When the feedback is focused on giving advice, the teacher, who had no part in developing the plan, has little motivation to make it succeed. The supervisor may give information by saying that many children went to the bathroom during the lesson. The teacher may respond explaining why this happened and how it could be corrected. When the supervisor states that the use of the bathroom must be restricted during the lesson, the teacher may ask what to do if a parent complains.

• The supervisor is giving information when a statement is made that, based on past behavior, John may cause some problems on the class trip. The teacher may have some ideas about how to deal with John to prevent his poor behavior. This is a far more effective means of dealing with the problem than for the supervisor to advise the teacher not to take John on the trip.

### Alternatives vs. One Best

• Discussing alternatives supplies an open-ended path to solutions. This approach encourages the teacher to think of different ways to do things. When the supervisor suggests there is only one best approach, the door is closed.

• The supervisor may have observed that the students had difficulty reading the questions on the chalkboard. The one best solution that the supervisor could offer is to put the questions on a ditto. The teacher may have several alternative suggestions. These may include writing larger, grouping the children closer to the board, reading the questions out loud, or dictating them to the youngsters.

### Based on Teacher Needs vs. Based on Supervisor Needs

• Motivating feedback focuses on the needs and interests of the teacher. The most positive improvements in teacher performance take place as a result of a teacher's awareness of, and discomfort with, a problem. A teacher who expresses a problem has a need to do something to correct or change that situation. Effective feedback will help that teacher by focusing on that expressed problem.

• The supervisor may believe that the problem he or she has identified is more important. This may well be true. But, there is little chance that the teacher will effectively work on the supervisor's problem until that teacher's problem has been resolved.

## Effective Feedback Clarifies, While Ineffective Feedback Confuses

### Paraphrasing vs. Misunderstanding

• Clarifying feedback ensures that what is said is understood. Paraphrasing can clarify feedback and prevent misunderstanding in two ways: (1) when you are not sure you understand what the teacher is saying, and (2) when you think the teacher may not understand or mean what he or she is saying. Paraphrasing is actually summarizing what you hear. The phrases that follow are easy leads to paraphrasing:

*"Are you saying ...?"*

*"Do you mean ...?"*

*"You seem to think..."*

*"What I hear is..."*

*"You lead me to believe that..."*

• Paraphrasing may also be useful in slowing down a conference that is moving too fast to be effective. It gives the teacher and the supervisor a chance to catch their breaths before moving on again.

• It is possible to guide the direction that a conference is taking by paraphrasing those parts of the conversation that lead where you want to go. You have then focused on one aspect and can encourage the teacher to discuss that part rather than others that are not important to the conference.

### Perception Check vs. Lack of Agreement

• Perception checking ensures that the teacher understands and is agreeing to the same set of ideas that the supervisor is. It checks that the teacher heard what the supervisor said. Perception checking actually encourages the teacher to summarize what the supervisor said or what the final agreed-upon plan is to be. Some leads to perception checking follow:

*"Tell me what you have outlined."*

*"What are the steps in your plan?"*

*"Let's review what we have agreed upon."*

*"How will you begin?"*

*"Is the plan clear to you?"*

• Perception checking provides insurance that both the teacher and the supervisor have a common understanding.

Figure 21-1 summarizes the guidelines for transmitting feedback.

## FORMING AN ACTION PLAN

Transmitting effective feedback results in the formation of a specific action plan designed to improve the teacher's performance. How much control you wish to have over the conference that forms that action plan is determined by your philosophy or style of leadership. The chart below illustrates two extreme styles of leadership. Few people are purely one style or another. Most people have aspects of both. Examine the "Leadership Style Chart" (Figure 21-2) to find yourself.

## Figure 21-1

---

### GUIDELINES FOR TRANSMITTING FEEDBACK

| EFFECTIVE FEEDBACK: | INEFFECTIVE FEEDBACK: |
|---|---|
| **Is Objective** | **Is Subjective** |
| observation | assumption |
| description | evaluation |
| | |
| **Is Realistic** | **Is Idealistic** |
| concrete | abstract |
| manageable | impossible |
| changeable | fixed |
| current | past |
| | |
| **Is Motivating** | **Is Demanding** |
| giving information | giving advice |
| alternatives | one best |
| based on teacher needs | based on supervisor needs |
| | |
| **Clarifies** | **Confuses** |
| paraphrasing | misunderstanding |
| perception check | lack of agreement |

---

## Level of Control

The role the supervisor plays during the conference determines who controls the formation of the action plan to improve teacher performance. The choice of role varies from the two extremes (total teacher dominance or total supervisor dominance) to a middle ground of working together.

There are five possible levels of control for the action plan conference:

1. **Total teacher dominance.** The supervisor receives teacher input and says little or nothing. Rather, the supervisor nods, smiles, and listens as the teacher discusses, elaborates, and determines.

SAMPLE LANGUAGE: *body language, reassuring attitude.*

2. **Teacher dominance.** The supervisor offers reflections and information. The supervisor contributes supporting data and additional information based on the direction in which the teacher is going.

SAMPLE LANGUAGE: *"I have read about..." "Recent research supports..." "I have observed that very..." "I agree that..." "That was successful..."*

**Figure 21-2**

---

### LEADERSHIP STYLE CHART

| ANALYTICAL/INCREMENTAL | GLOBAL/INTUITIVE |
|---|---|
| I... | I... |
| rely on myself | ask for input |
| am a realist | am creative |
| deal with the concrete | deal with the abstract |
| push others | allow others to push me |
| like quiet, being alone | am social, like interrelationships |
| rely on proven techniques | try new ideas |
| am logical | am intuitive |
| set deadlines | am flexible |
| conduct short conversations | prefer long discussions |
| deal with facts | deal with possibilities |
| am a thinking person | am a feeling person |
| make up my mind quickly | need time to deliberate |
| prefer stability | prefer change |
| like being with those I know | like meeting new people |
| am a talker | am a listener |
| am unemotional | am emotional |

---

3. **Collaboration.** The teacher and supervisor jointly solve a problem. Both the teacher and supervisor contribute alternatives, possible plans, and suggested solutions to the stated problem.

> SAMPLE LANGUAGE: *"Have you thought about ...?" "It may help to..." "Other aspects may include..." "How about ...?" "Let's turn that around and..."*

4. **Supervisor dominance.** The supervisor presents suggestions and alternatives for problem solving. The teacher participates in the selection of one of the alternatives.

> SAMPLE LANGUAGE: *"Which of these appears better ...?" "Here are two ways of..." "The best solutions are..." "You should try one of these..." "How about these ...?"*

5. **Total supervisor dominance.** The supervisor gives directions. The supervisor selects the one best plan and gives details of how to accomplish it.

> SAMPLE LANGUAGE: *"You should..." "Here are the steps to take..." "Within two weeks, you..." "First of all..."*

## Selecting a Level of Control

Although personal leadership style is a powerful factor in selecting a comfortable level of control for the action plan conference, there is a second factor or consideration, that is, teacher competence. Teachers who are mature, dedicated, creative, and experienced, obviously require less control than teachers who are inexperienced, disinterested, or unmotivated. Both factors will direct your selection of the proper level of control for each teacher's action plan conference. (See Section 4 for a complete discussion of teacher types and the attitudes and perceptions that identify them.)

Figure 21-3 summarizes the factors that affect the selection of a level of control.

**Figure 21-3**

---

**Factors That Affect the Selection of a Level of Control**

Levels of Control

| Teacher Control | | Joint Control | | Supervisor Control |
|---|---|---|---|---|
| **1** | **2** | **△3** | **4** | **5** |
| **Level of Control** | | **Leadership Style** | | **Teacher Type** |
| 1. Total Teacher Dominance | | Strong Global | | Master |
| 2. Teacher Dominance | | Mostly Global | | Outstanding |
| 3. Collaboration | | Global/Analytical | | Good |
| 4. Supervisor Dominance | | Mostly Analytical | | Has Potential |
| 5. Total Supervisor Dominance | | Strong Analytical | | Inexperienced |

---

## THE SIX STAGES OF CONFERENCING

Successful conferences usually move through six stages. Remember, two important factors that must be considered as you move through each stage are (1) the use of effective feedback, and (2) the selection of a level of control appropriate to your leadership style and the type of teacher with whom you are conferencing.

The basic goal of any conference is to improve teacher performance. Although it is necessary to move through all six stages, the time needed for each stage will vary. The differences in time needed depend on three factors: (1) the nature of the conference goal, (2) the type of teacher with whom you are conferencing, and (3) your leadership style.

There are also several details you should keep in mind when planning a conference:

1. Conduct the conference as soon as possible after the observation when memories of the events are fresh both in your mind and in the teacher's.

2. A 20- to 30-minute conference is most effective. A longer conference is usually very tiring, while a shorter conference does not permit sufficient expression of ideas.

3. Hold the conference in a private and quiet setting. Avoid interruptions that disrupt the conversation and train of thought, waste valuable time, and make the teacher think he or she is not important. Avoid sitting at your desk, as it is an intimidating symbol.

4. Set the climate by greeting the teacher and thanking him or her for coming. Say something positive, either personally or professionally.

Figure 21-4 summarizes the six stages of conferencing. Each stage is described in detail below.

## Stage 1: Identify the Conference Goal

The identification of the goal gives the conference a clear focus. Both the supervisor and the teacher are aware of why they are meeting and what will be discussed. This understanding sets the stage for effective and efficient use of conference time.

The following are Stage 1's sample language and the particular level of control in parentheses:

*"What is your goal for this conference?"* (Total teacher dominance)

*"How do you think the lesson went?"* (Teacher dominance)

*"First you state your views and then I will give you my views of the lesson."* (Collaboration)

*"These are the parts of the lesson we need to share ideas about."* (Supervisor dominance)

*"This is the part of the lesson we need to discuss."* (Total supervisor dominance)

## Stage 2: Review Gathered Data

All important information should be reviewed during this stage. The data should be objective, observable, and descriptive. It should also be realistic, concrete, manageable, changeable, and current. Avoid the negative effects of ineffective feedback. The purpose of this review is to identify the problem that will become the area of focus for improvement.

**Figure 21-4**

---

### THE SIX STAGES OF CONFERENCING

| STAGE | OBJECTIVE |
|---|---|
| 1. Identify the conference goal | To give the conference a focus |
| 2. Review gathered data | To identify the problems |
| 3. Select an area of focus for improvement | To focus improvement efforts on one specific problem |
| 4. Explore alternative actions | To look at various ways of improving teacher performance in the area of focus |
| 5. Form an action plan | To select one alternative and use that to develop a detailed plan for improvement |
| 6. Confirm understanding | To ensure that what the supervisor said and what the teacher said are clearly understood by both |

---

The following are Stage 2's sample language and the particular level of control in parentheses:

"*What aspects of the lesson do you want to discuss?*" (Total teacher dominance)

"*What parts of the lesson were not as effective as you would have liked?*" (Teacher dominance)

"*Let's compare our views about which parts of the lesson could be improved.*" (Collaboration)

*"Here are some of the problems I saw. How did you see these?"* (Supervisor dominance)

*"These are the reasons you had trouble with the lesson."* (Total supervisor dominance)

## Stage 3: Select an Area of Focus for Improvement

The review of the data may identify various problems that could be worked on, so select one area or one group of related areas to work on at one time. This is done because no one can concentrate on too many priorities at the same time. If your objective is to really help a teacher improve, be realistic about how much can be done effectively. Also remember that teacher motivation is the key to improvement. You may have to balance your preference of the area of focus with the teacher's interest.

The following are Stage 3's sample language and the particular level of control in parentheses:

*"What area are you interested in working on?"* (Total teacher dominance)

*"Which of the areas you discussed do you want to focus on?"* (Teacher dominance)

*"We have discussed three areas of focus. Which one will you focus on?"* (Collaboration)

*"I have shown you two areas that need to be worked on. Which is your priority?"* (Supervisor dominance)

*"This is the most important problem. Let's work on it."* (Total supervisor dominance)

## Stage 4: Explore Alternative Actions

Usually there are several ways in which improvement can be made. The purpose of this stage is to explore those alternatives. The variety of approaches should be fully discussed so that the one best approach for that teacher and that class becomes the action plan. This is a time to be creative and explore multiple ideas.

The following are Stage 4's sample language and the particular level of control in parentheses:

*"What are your ideas for improvement?"* (Total teacher dominance)

*"I have some research information that may help you explore many ways to reach your goal."* (Teacher dominance)

*"Let's compare the alternatives each of us thinks will bring you to your goal."* (Collaboration)

*"Here are two ways to reach your improvement goal. Which one seems more appropriate to you?"* (Supervisor dominance)

*"Of all the ways in which this area can be improved, this is the best one for your situation."* (Total supervisor dominance)

## Stage 5: Form an Action Plan

After all the alternatives for improvement have been explored, one best alternative is selected. That alternative becomes the basis of an action plan, which is then discussed in detail. Figure 21-5 shows a sample action plan, showing the plan details and implementation steps.

The following are Stage 5's sample language and the particular level of control in parentheses:

*"What are the details of your plan?"* (Total teacher dominance)

*"How can I help you with your plan?"* (Teacher dominance)

*"Let's form a plan together."* (Collaboration)

*"Here are some suggested plans. Which is most comfortable for you?"* (Supervisor dominance)

*"I will outline a specific plan for you to follow."* (Total supervisor dominance)

## Stage 6: Confirm Understanding

The purpose of the confirmation stage is to make sure that what you said and what the teacher said are clearly understood. This action is well worth the time because the clearer the understanding, the better the chances for success. Confirming understanding is achieved by two techniques previously discussed in this section, that is, paraphrasing and perception checking. These techniques should be used with consideration for the level of control selected and the type of teacher with whom you are working. For example, with total teacher dominance, neither is necessary. When working with total supervisor dominance, both may be worthwhile.

The following are Stage 6's sample language and the particular level of control in parentheses:

**When Confirmation Is Unnecessary**
*Reassure with a nod and a smile.* (Total teacher dominance)

*Reassure with a supportive statement, such as "Your plan reflects the results of current research. That is . . ."* (Teacher dominance)

**When Confirmation Is Necessary**
Paraphrasing—*"This is my understanding of our action plan."* (Collaboration)

Figure 21-5

## SAMPLE ACTION PLAN

| Plan Details | Plan Implementation |
|---|---|
| 1. Set the plan objective. | To improve students' ability to write expressive compositions. |
| 2. Outline the action:<br>what to do | Provide a common experience about which all of the students can write. |
| how to do it | Take the children on a trip to a local zoo to observe the habitats of the animals. |
| | The students will take notes about what they observe. |
| | They will use their notes and specific guide questions to write a first draft. |
| | Suggestions for improvement will be given by the teacher and peers. |
| | The compositions will be rewritten. |
| | The rewritten compositions will be evaluated. |
| when to do it | On Monday, prepare the students for the trip. Discuss differences in habitats. |
| | Give the students questions to guide their observation. |
| | Take the trip the following Monday. |
| 3. State expected results. | Within one month's time, the students will improve their ability to write expressive compositions. |
| 4. Specify responsibilities. | Teacher—To follow through on all the specified details. |
| | To report results using students' written work in one month. |
| | Supervisor—To assist the teacher in planning the trip. |
| | To visit the class during the teacher/peer evaluation stage. |
| | To review results with the teacher in one month. |

Perception checking— *"What is your understanding of the action plan?"* (Collaboration)

Paraphrasing— *"I believe that this is the action plan you selected."* (Supervisor dominance)

Perception checking— *"How would you describe that action plan?"* (Supervisor dominance)

Paraphrasing—*"Let me summarize the action plan you will follow."* (Total supervisor dominance)

Perception checking—*"Please outline the action plan that you will take so that we are both sure we understand what is to be done."* (Total supervisor dominance)

# Writing Effective Communications

Have you ever felt as if you were drowning in a sea of paper? Indeed, written messages have become a daily and essential part of how we communicate about everything we do. Yet the written word is a demon that can trip you up!

Since your written message depends on its reader for interpretation, be aware there are three problems that can arise here:

1. Subtle clues, hidden in the words we assume are neutral, can cause emotional reactions.
2. Outside influences, at the time of the reading, can cause misinterpretations.
3. A lack of clarity can confuse the reader.

This section will help you deal with these three problems by presenting strategies for writing effective and humane communications.

## THE STRENGTHS AND WEAKNESSES OF WRITTEN COMMUNICATION

Written communication is in constant use because it serves several purposes:

1. The written words permanently record the message. Once the words are set on paper, they are indisputable.

2. A written message may clarify, explain, direct, or guide a complicated process. When a series of actions is required, the best way to transfer that information is in writing.

3. Written messages may be kept and reread for recall and clarity.

There are, however, several weaknesses to consider about written communication:

1. Written messages are thoughts frozen on paper. Once recorded, they cannot be retracted.

2. The written message offers no clarification or modification beyond the specific words stated.

3. Written communications do not provide the benefits of verbal and nonverbal information and explanation.

## WRITING FOR THE INTENDED READER

As you write, keep the following points in mind.

### Attitudes of Self-Worth and Esteem

Members of your staff vary in the degree of security they feel. (See Section 20 for a complete discussion of this concept.) Your communication can enhance or diminish those feelings. Consider the way you word your communication. Words that are nonthreatening to a secure staff member may strike terror in those with low self-worth and esteem. Staff members who are easily threatened should receive only communications inviting them to a conference.

Communications can be made less threatening by including possible causes and solutions for the issue. Figure 22-1 illustrates a communication of this type.

Negative communications can be softened by first stating all available data and then drawing inferences both positive and negative. Figure 22-2 offers an illustrative sample.

### Positive Orientation

Including positive comments in your written communications allows the reader to believe that he or she is valued, competent, and important. This positive approach is

**Figure 22-1**

---

**Sample—Letter stating causes and solutions**

Dear Mr. Smith,

This letter summarizes our discussion about your concerns for several students who have not made satisfactory progress in reading.

There are several causes for this problem:

1. Some of the students have a limited English background and hear only a language other than English at home.
2. Some of the students are new admissions to the school and lack a strong reading skills background.
3. Some of the students lack many skills necessary for progress.

There are several suggested solutions you should try to help these students:

1. Assign an English-speaking buddy to each non-English-speaking youngster to provide an English language model and to clarify what otherwise may be confusing.
2. Review the records of the new admissions to determine their former achievement.
3. Conduct a reading assessment of each student and record skill lacks. Group the students according to skill needs and teach those skills. Assign independent activities for review and reinforcement.

---

essential in maintaining your relationship with the staff member. It serves your purposes to be viewed as helpful, considerate, and humane.

Positive comments may refer to the staff member's successful past performance, positive attitude, or personal life. Figure 22-3 shows sample comments with a positive orientation. An appropriate statement of this type should be used to complete the letters in Figures 22-1 and 22-2.

# WRITING WITH A PURPOSE

If your purposeful writing is to be truly effective in the school setting, keep in mind the following considerations.

### Figure 22-2

**Sample—Letter stating data and inferences (positive and negative)**

Dear Ms. Gilmore,

My purpose in writing this letter is to bring your repeated lateness to your attention. An examination of your time card documents that you have been late, from three to fifteen minutes, twelve times in the last seventeen days. Your time cards for the previous two months show a similar pattern. In September, you were late ten out of fourteen days. In October, you were late seventeen out of twenty-two days.

Your lateness may be caused by:

1. Extraordinary traffic conditions
2. Problems with your car
3. Unexpected family problems that demand attention
4. Personal health problems
5. Starting your chores too late in the morning

However, your lateness:

1. Leaves your class unattended
2. Causes you to rush and therefore enter the classroom in an anxious state
3. Prevents you from preparing for the day's work
4. Limits your ability to reinforce early morning routines

### Figure 22-3

**Sample—Positive comments for letter conclusion**

You are to be commended for your attention to, and concern with, the progress of all of your students.

Your efforts and results have always been of the highest caliber.

It is always a pleasure to work with you. I look forward to our joint efforts on this new project.

Congratulations on the graduation of your son. I join you in joy and pride for his accomplishments.

## Length of the Communication

The length of a communication reflects the delicate balance between being long enough to be clear and short enough to be concise and focused. One important consideration in determining the length of the communication is the reader's familiarity with the subject. Those readers who have experience and background in the subject will naturally require less explanation than those who do not.

The communication length is also dependent upon its purpose. It is a waste of time to write a letter when a note or short memo can send the message. On the other hand, a note cannot provide a detailed explanation or the specifics of a plan that are better placed in a letter.

## Purpose of the Communication

Communication serves a variety of purposes. A short note or memo may serve as a reminder, a confirmation of an appointment or agreement, or an invitation to a conference.

A letter is probably the better communicator to respond negatively to a request but include an explanation, ask or answer a question, record a summary of actions, give detailed instructions or directions, or clarify a plan.

## Clarity of the Communication

The degree of clarity required of the communication will vary with several factors. First of all, set the stage at the start of the communication. Establish your role, the reader's role, and the purpose of the communication.

When writing to a member of your staff, it may not always be necessary to establish your role. It is understood that you are the supervisor and that you are writing to them from that point of view. When you are writing to someone outside of your immediate staff, it may be very important to state who you are at the outset. Figure 22-4 shows an example of a situation where it was important to establish the supervisor's role.

The reader's role and the purpose of the communication should become obvious in the first few sentences. Figures 22-1, 22-2 and 22-4 all state the purpose of the communication in the first sentence. The role of the reader, or what is required of him or her, becomes obvious before the letter has been completed.

When the message is not as obvious, it may be important to state "My purpose in writing this letter is..." and "Your role in this problem is as follows..." Those definitive statements cannot be misinterpreted.

**Figure 22-4**

---

**Sample—Letter establishing supervisor's role**

Dear Mr. Burton,

As principal of the school, my purpose in writing to you is to respond to the request you made of the classroom teacher for special meals for your son. The teacher gave your letter to me since she could not provide an answer.

---

The next important clarity factor deals with the reader's familiarity with the subject. For example, in Figure 22-1, it is not necessary to include a discussion of the importance of reading skills in the letter. The teacher is obviously aware of that because he brought the problem to you. In Figure 22-2, it is also not necessary to remind the teacher about the exact time when she is considered late. Obviously, that is the topic of the letter.

At other times, however, it may be important to consider the reader's lack of background and experience. An extensive explanation may be required for the reader to understand the intent of the letter. When possible, it may be advisable to attach that background information to the letter and make reference to it rather than include it in the body of the letter. Figure 22-5 shows how this may be done.

**Figure 22-5**

---

**Sample—Letter containing separate background information sheet**

Dear Mrs. Daily,

As principal of the school, my purpose in writing to you is to present the dangerous security problem we face in this school. A five-year history of correspondence about this matter is attached for your information.

---

The last important clarity factor is concerned with the use of precise words that send the message you desire clearly, succinctly, and precisely. Examine the following pairs of sentences that show effective and ineffective use of words on the same topic:

## Words Used Effectively

1. **clear**
   The stated curriculum for your grade includes a unit on literature.

2. **friendly**
   I am delighted that our conference gave us an opportunity to chat about several matters.

3. **thoughtful**
   I have given consideration to your proposal and have reached a decision.

4. **specific**
   The problem may be resolved by assigning reliable monitors the tasks of distribution and collection.

5. **important**
   Students should be sent out of the room with a pass or a written note.

6. **logical**
   Before using the new material preview it and discuss it with other teachers on the grade.

7. **concrete**
   Positive behavior modification techniques have proven to be very effective discipline strategies.

8. **pleasant**
   Your difficulty in using the overhead projector was probably due to a lack of experience with this instructional device.

9. **focused**
   This action is harmful and should not be continued.

10. **focused**
    This action is harmful and should not be continued.

## Words Used Ineffectively

1. **vague**
   The grade's curriculum provides for variety and balance.

2. **impersonal**
   Several of your concerns were discussed during our conference.

3. **arbitrary**
   Your proposal is not accepted.

4. **general**
   The problem is concerned with classroom management.

5. **trivial**
   Use the correct form when sending an ill child to the office.

6. **illogical**
   Use the new material in your next lesson.

7. **abstract**
   Youngsters require security and acceptance to be able to function in a group.

8. **insulting**
   Using a machine you know nothing about was a stupid move that resulted in disaster.

9. **wordy**
   Although this has not happened before, even though it is always more likely to occur again once such a pattern has happened, it is important to both know and understand that this action, without exception, cannot continue.

10. **curt**
    Stop this action immediately.

Now, judge your use of precise words in written communication. Compare your communications with the grouped descriptors above.

Figure 22-6 may be used as a reminder for making your communication more effective.

**Figure 22-6**

---

**Guide to Effective Written Communication**

**Reduce Anxiety:**    1. State causes and propose solutions

    2. State all data and draw inferences

    3. Include positive comments

**Write Purposefully:**    1. Select the appropriate length

    2. Match the length to the purpose

**Clarify:**    1. Establish: your role

        the reader's role

        the purpose of the communication

    2. Consider background data required by the reader

    3. Use precise words

# Keeping Track of What You Are Doing

You communicate effectively with yourself when you keep accurate records about the what, when, why, and with whom of your activities. These records serve to guide you in setting goals, making suggestions, and monitoring progress.

## HOW TO RECORD INFORMATION

There are various ways to record the important aspects of your supervisory activities. Each has its place and should be used appropriately in each individual situation.

### Formal Records

Formal records are written records that require the teacher's signature and are placed in the teacher's file. They become a part of a growing body of information about the teacher.

The teacher's file, as an official collection of data, is subject to specific requirements:

1. Everything in the file must be signed by the teacher.
2. The teacher must have a copy of everything in the file.
3. The file is open to the teacher's inspection.

Data appropriate for formal records includes appropriately signed forms discussed in previous sections. A list of these forms follows:

1. Exploration Conference Summary
2. Classroom Environment Observation Form
3. Time-on-Task Review
4. Formal Exploration Observations:
        Pre-Observation Plan
        Observation Write-Up
5. Intensive Guided Supervision:
        Plan Specification
        Review of Post-Visit Conference
6. Collaborative Supervision:
        Plan Specification
        Plan Review
7. Peer Supervision:
        Plan Specification
        Plan Review
8. Self-Directed Supervision:
        Plan Specification
        Plan Review
9. Supervision Summary

This formal accumulation of data, however, provides no opportunity to record and maintain records about material not kept in the teacher's official file. That is the purpose of informal records.

## Informal Records

There are three types of data appropriate for informal records. These include:

1. Your private notes, reactions, thoughts, and projections about both formal and informal supervisory efforts
2. Reminders, due dates, requests made, suggestions given, books loaned, and reported data
3. Ongoing diagnostic data that may not be signed by the teacher and is therefore informal, such as Level-of-Effectiveness Assessment (see Section 4), Plan

Review Memo (see Section 7), Memo Re Informal Visit (see Section 8), and Top Sheet for Student Product Review (see Section 11).

## HOW TO KEEP INFORMAL RECORDS

There is no one best way to keep informal records. You must decide what works best for you. Some suggestions to help you get started are given here.

### Use a Looseleaf Binder

The binder should contain an individual page for each teacher. This page is best kept as a data log. (See Figure 23-1.) Dated entries should be made regarding private thoughts, reminders, and suggestions made to the teacher. These may then be used as the specifics for follow-up.

In addition, the supervisory forms kept as informal data should be placed behind the individual log page. This data includes diagnostic information that should not be included in the teacher's file because it is not signed. The informal data provides support information and reminders about teacher needs.

**What to Record.**  The individual data log serves as a quick summary and reminder. An entry should be made about each diagnostic assessment and teacher interaction that is significant. The entries include the date and form of the data. The comment and personal notes you make are your guides to future actions.

**How to Remember the Data.**  The dated details you have noted on the logs may be remembered by recording them on a monthly overview calendar. (See Figure 23-2.) Keeping the calendar open on your desk will help you keep track of your plans on a daily basis.

### Use Separate Teacher Files

A separate and individual file may be used as an alternative means of collecting informal data and recording notes. The file would include the same information suggested for the looseleaf binder.

### Use Files According to Topic

You may prefer to keep topic-specific records together rather than place informal supervisory data behind the individual teacher's log page. For example, you might keep

**Figure 23-1**

## INDIVIDUAL DATA LOG

**Teacher's Name** K. Hudson    **Assignment** 4-201    **Year** 19xx–19xx

| DATE | FORM OF THE DATA | COMMENT | NOTE |
|------|------------------|---------|------|
| 9/23 | Exploration Conference | Difficulty in maintaining discipline with three disruptive students | Schedule a meeting with the guidance counselor and the teacher to plan a behavior modification program |
| 10/21 | Informal Visit | Three students are having difficulty with addition with exchange | Teacher memo to order squared material |
| 11/4 | Plan Review Memo | Only two mathematics lessons are planned for the week | Check mathematics plans for the week of 11/10 |
| 11/19 | Teacher Talk | Teacher stated that the behavior modification plan is going well | |

Figure 23-2

## SAMPLE OVERVIEW CALENDAR

# October

| Sun | Mon | Tue | Wed | Thu | Fri | Sat |
|-----|-----|-----|-----|-----|-----|-----|
| | | | 1 | 2 | 3 | 4 |
| 5 | 6<br>9:45 – exploration conference with S. Masters | 7 | 8<br>K. Hudson – check use of squared materials | 9 | 10<br>1st floor – check early A.M. routine | 11 |
| 12 | 13<br>K. Hudson – check math plans | 14 | 15<br>9:30 – classroom environment observation of L. Lindsey | 16<br>Class 3 – 105 check hall behavior | 17 | 18 |
| 19 | 20<br>Informal visits – grade 2 | 21<br>10:00 – time-on-task review of P. Romoff | 22<br>10:30 – formal observation of 5 – 205 | 23 | 24<br>2nd floor – check 3 P.M. dismissal | 25 |
| 26 | 27<br>9:45 supervisory conference with A. Winden | 28 | 29 | 30 | 31 | |

one looseleaf binder for all plan review memos sent, arranging them alphabetically. A second binder or file folder might contain all top sheets for student product reviews.

The advantage of maintaining topic-specific records is to allow you to easily compare progress and quality of instruction between and among teachers with similar assignments. For example, you could review all student writing product review top sheets for the fourth grade, or you could compare how plan reviews of the science and social studies departments demonstrate efforts toward the objective of teaching reading in the content areas.

Topic-specific records are a disadvantage when you want to review the progress of individual teachers by monitoring ongoing data. You would need to pull at least three sets of data to conduct this review: individual teacher logs, collectively kept plan review memos, and top sheets for student product review.

## FINDING THE TIME TO PERFORM ALL YOUR DUTIES

Time is a precious and important commodity. It cannot be made up, stored, or stopped. Because you have an infinite set of roles and responsibilities to accomplish within a finite time frame, the use of time is a major consideration.

### Use Time Effectively

Efficient and effective use of time is realized when you set personal goals. This will help you get maximum benefits from time expended. Four suggested personal goals follow:

- *Personal Example*. Demonstrate caring through sincere and tactful treatment of staff. Show sympathetic concern for both professional and personal problems. Provide positive reinforcement at every opportunity by complimenting good work and workers.
- *Be Precise*. Send clear communications. Do not leave a staff member guessing what you mean or want. Clarify individual goals agreed upon.
- *Model Time Efficiency*. Provide an efficient and effective model for use of time. Avoid appearing harassed, breathless, or out of patience.
- Help People Help Each Other. Make good use of peer instructors and teacher models. Use teacher-to-teacher conferences and visits.

**Figure 23-3**

## Time Frame for Daily Activity

8:00 - 8:40    Conduct:
short talks with staff members
notifications to staff members
reminders for staff members
short group meetings with staff members

9:00 - 9:15    Record:
student entry behavior
morning classroom routines
student use of early morning time

Period Breaks    Note:
movement of groups and individual students through the halls

9:30 - 11:30    Observe Instruction:
informal visits to classrooms
classroom environment observation
formal observation of direct instruction
time-on-task review
teacher conferences during preparation periods

11:30 - 12:00    Noninstructional Activities:
administrative paper work
return telephone calls
review diagnostic information

12:00 - 1:00    Monitor:
efficiency of kitchen personnel
student attention to lunchroom rules
performance of teacher(s) on duty
performance of other assigned personnel

1:00 - 1:30    Noninstructional Activities:
see 11:30 - 12:00 above

1:30 - 2:30    Observe Instruction:
see 9:30 - 11:30 above

2:30 - 3:00    Record:
student dismissal behavior
closing routines

3:00 - 3:30    Conduct:
see 8:00 - 8:40 above

3:30 - 5:00    Noninstructional Activities:
see 11:30 - 12:00 above

## Allocate Time Effectively

When time is effectively allocated, it is efficiently used. Time should be allocated for individual supervisory work, day-to-day supervision, and administrative chores.

Individual supervisory plans (discussed in Part III) matched to diagnosed teacher needs (discussed in Part II) benefit everyone. Each teacher receives the benefits of your time and attention in relation to the supervisory plan. Weak or inexperienced teachers require, and therefore receive, a large allocation of your time in intensive guided supervision. More able teachers receive a lesser, but still essential, allocation of your time in collaborative supervisory plans. Very able teachers receive small, but significant, allocations of your time in peer or self-directed supervisory plans. Everyone receives a differentiated allocation of your time according to their needs and specified goals.

Time allocated for day-to-day supervisory activities, targeted at both monitoring efforts and diagnosing needs, is used most effectively if scheduled during optimum time frames. Consider the best time of day to conduct specific activities and plan your day accordingly. At times, your time frame plans will work smoothly. At other times, they may be made impossible by unanticipated mandates and crisis situations. In either case, you use time most effectively when you plan ahead and record what you will do during specific time frames. A sample time frame for a day's activities is given in Figure 23-3; it can be modified to fit your individual situation.

Also, your use of allocated time will vary with the time of the year. In general, diagnostic supervisory efforts targeted at the selection of a supervisory plan are best conducted early in the school year. Testing and pre-vacation time frames are best used to monitor teacher efforts. Consideration of results and progress made toward objectives are optimally conducted late in the school year.

# How to Supervise Others Who Teach

# Supervising Teacher Assistants

Supervision of instruction should be concerned with everyone who plays a part in the instructional life of students. Thus far, we have discussed the professionally prepared and licensed teacher. There are, however, others who instruct students, with or without even minimal preparation. Since their work impacts on students, it is important to consider their roles, their expectations, and their supervision.

Many school districts provide support service to the professional teacher by employing teacher assistants. The terms used to identify this support position vary with the district and, at times, with the level of preparation required. The job title may be: paraprofessional, educational assistant, teacher aide, assistant teacher, or teacher assistant.

## CRITERIA FOR EMPLOYING TEACHER ASSISTANTS

Some school districts use this employment opportunity to benefit low income groups in the community. This is especially true in large urban areas.

**235**

## Preparation Required

The required level of preparation differs from district to district. Most districts require a high school diploma; others may require six college credits in education. Participants may be allowed to work while they complete those required college credits. Some districts offer career ladder opportunities and may even pay the college tuition and provide released time for attendance at the courses.

## Program Placement

Teacher assistants provide support instructional services under the direct supervision of a professional teacher. They are usually assigned to primary grade classes, classes with large registers, special education classes, English second language classes, and remediation programs.

# THE ROLES OF THE TEACHER ASSISTANT, THE TEACHER, AND THE SUPERVISOR

The teacher assistant, professional teacher, and supervisor each play a different and significant role in making this support service effective.

## The Teacher Assistant

The role performed by the teacher assistant varies with the particular assignment and program placement. In general, however, teacher assistants are responsible for both management and instructional tasks, as outlined here:

1. Management Tasks
   a. Take attendance—Once attendance is taken by the teacher assistant, it should be reported to the teacher who will record the data in the official attendance book, card, or register. The assistant teacher should not make entries on official documents.
   b. Decorate bulletin boards—Although the teacher assistant may physically mount the display, the professional teacher determines the materials to be displayed, their location, and arrangement.
   c. Assist with breakfast/lunch programs—The teacher assistant helps students get their food, open packages and containers, dispose of trash, and maintain good behavior while eating.
   d. Assist students with outer clothing—The teacher assistant helps students with jackets, coats, boots, zippers, and buttons.

e. Transmit materials—The teacher assistant may pick up, return, deliver, and store materials of all types.

f. Maintain materials—The teacher assistant keeps the classroom materials neat, in good order, in appropriate areas, and ready for student use.

g. Prepare materials—The professional teacher instructs the teacher assistant about what materials to prepare, how to prepare them, and when the task is to be done.

h. Mark students' papers—The teacher assistant may correct students' work using guidelines established by the professional teacher. The results are then reported to the professional teacher, who reviews the results and evaluates the students' progress.

i. Assist in crisis intervention—The teacher assistant helps the professional teacher maintain order and control acting-out behavior.

2. **Instructional Tasks**

a. Tutor one-to-one—The professional teacher selects the student, material, and the type of instruction to be conducted by the teacher assistant.

b. Reinforce small-group work—The teacher assistant works with small groups to review and reinforce skills and concepts previously taught by the professional teacher. The professional teacher selects the members of the small group, the materials, and the instructional approach to be used.

c. Assist the teacher with instruction—The teacher assistant's instructional role is defined by the professional teacher in advance of the lesson. The assistance may include distributing materials, collecting materials, operating media, assisting individual students, or monitoring the activities of individual students.

3. **Inappropriate Tasks**

Since the teacher assistant is not professionally qualified or licensed, the following tasks should *not* be performed:

a. Administering standardized tests

b. Evaluating students

c. Making entries on official records

d. Teaching skills and concepts not previously taught

e. Supervising individuals or groups of youngsters without the professional teacher

Figure 24-1 provides a summary of the guidelines for the appropriate involvement of teacher assistants. These guidelines may be useful in providing clarification for both the teacher and the teacher assistant. The guidelines should be fully discussed and explained in terms of their application to individual situations.

## The Professional Teacher

The professional teacher is the key figure in the effective involvement of the teacher assistant. The teacher's responsibilities are to:

1. Transmit information—The professional teacher is responsible for informing the teacher assistant about all data that is important to the performance of his or her

**Figure 24-1**

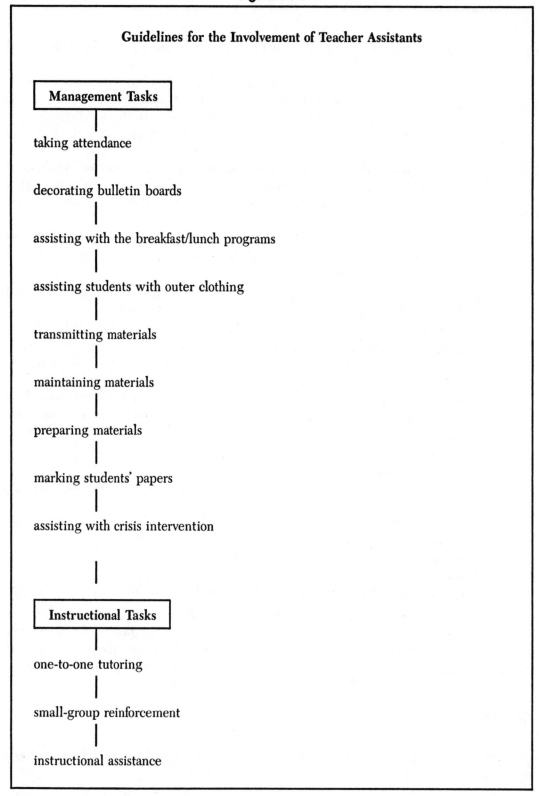

**Guidelines for the Involvement of Teacher Assistants**

**Management Tasks**

taking attendance

decorating bulletin boards

assisting with the breakfast/lunch programs

assisting students with outer clothing

transmitting materials

maintaining materials

preparing materials

marking students' papers

assisting with crisis intervention

**Instructional Tasks**

one-to-one tutoring

small-group reinforcement

instructional assistance

tasks. This information may include specifics about particular youngsters, materials, instructional techniques, and procedures.

2. Provide required training—The teacher assistant may require training before particular tasks can be undertaken. The areas that require training may include how to use particular materials, classroom management techniques, behavior modification program implementation, procedures for distribution and collection of materials, how to use particular media devices, how to check students' work, and how to report information to the teacher.

3. Assign appropriate tasks—Those tasks assigned to the teacher assistant should be within the stated guidelines provided in Figure 24-1.

4. Supervise teacher assistant activities—The professional teacher is responsible for the work of the teacher assistant. The professional teacher must be aware of both what and how the teacher assistant performs. When the performance can be improved, the professional teacher must bring this to the attention of the teacher assistant and provide the training required.

In short, the professional teacher directs what, how, when, where, and with whom the teacher assistant works.

## The Supervisor

The supervisor assumes the responsibility for the effectiveness of a learning environment that includes both a professional teacher and a teacher assistant. The supervisor's role is to:

1. Promote a positive interaction between the professional and the teacher assistant—An assessment of the quality of the interaction may be made through formal and informal visits to the learning environment, formal and informal discussions with the teacher and the teacher assistant, and observation of the teacher and teacher assistant in relaxed settings (such as the teacher's lunchroom, the halls, before and after session).

2. Determine the appropriate use of the teacher assistant's services—A determination of the appropriateness of use of the teacher assistant's services is best made through personal observation of the teacher assistant in the performance of tasks.

3. Assess the performance of the teacher assistant in consultation with the professional teacher—An assessment of the performance of the teacher assistant should be conducted by the professional teacher with consideration for the input of the teacher assistant. This assessment should be presented and discussed with you.

Improvement in any of the areas stated above may be accomplished through interaction with the professional teacher and/or interaction with the teacher assistant.

**Interaction With the Professional Teacher.** The professional teacher may need some assistance in appreciating and understanding how to fully use the services of a teacher assistant. Specifically, the teacher may need your help in developing the ability to:

1. Motivate the work of the teacher assistant through the use of praise
2. Define and clarify the particular tasks to be accomplished
3. Identify appropriate tasks to be assigned
4. Explain and discuss both what and why tasks are assigned
5. Monitor the activities performed

**Interaction With the Teacher Assistant.** Your direct involvement with the teacher assistant may help to:

1. Improve the quality of the interaction between the adults
2. Clarify the standards required of all staff members
3. Establish the role of the professional teacher
4. Reinforce the role defined for the teacher assistant
5. Encourage an improvement in performance

## ASSESSING THE TEACHER ASSISTANT

Figure 24-2 supplies a list of criteria for the performance of the teacher assistant. These criteria may be useful when an assessment is conducted. The criteria included are grouped into two categories: (1) personal characteristics, and (2) role-related tasks.

### Personal Characteristics

The criteria in this category deal with the personality and attitude of the teacher assistant. Specifically, they include the social, emotional, and physical aspects of the individual. In addition, they intend to target the assistant's ability to deal with individual academic, emotional, and physical differences that may be found within a group of students, school personnel, and parents. These items may be very important if the teacher assistant is assigned to a special education program. The criteria also attempt to include attitudes of respect for and rapport with school personnel, students, and parents. In essence, this involves the way in which the assistant acts, interacts, and relates to others. Other criteria focus on the individual's degree of cooperation with

Figure 24-2

## CRITERIA FOR THE PERFORMANCE OF TEACHER ASSISTANTS

Name _____  Assignment _____  Date _____

Scale: O = outstanding   G = good   S = satisfactory   NI = needs improvement   U = unsatisfactory

Signatures: _____(teacher)   _____(teacher assistant)

| ITEMS PERSONAL CHARACTERISTICS | RATING | COMMENTS |
|---|---|---|
| Demonstrates: | | |
| social and emotional stability | _____ | _____ |
| physical stamina | _____ | _____ |
| acceptance of individual differences | _____ | _____ |
| respect for school personnel | _____ | _____ |
| respect for pupils | _____ | _____ |
| respect for parents | _____ | _____ |
| rapport with school personnel | _____ | _____ |
| rapport with pupils | _____ | _____ |
| rapport with parents | _____ | _____ |
| a cooperative attitude | _____ | _____ |
| good judgment | _____ | _____ |
| acceptance of criticism | _____ | _____ |
| acceptance of assignments | _____ | _____ |
| **ROLE-RELATED TASKS** | | |
| completes assignments | _____ | _____ |
| takes responsibility | _____ | _____ |
| follows directions | _____ | _____ |
| performs tasks | _____ | _____ |
| attendance | _____ | _____ |
| punctuality | _____ | _____ |

requests made of him or her. In addition, the criterion of good judgment is intended to estimate how the individual reacts to unforeseeable situations. The areas of acceptance of criticism and assignments are targeted at determining the degree to which the individual can deal with directions given.

## Role-Related Tasks

This category deals with the delivery system of assigned tasks. Items specifically included intend to assess how well the individual completes what is asked of him or her and takes responsibility for actions performed. Also assessed are how directions are followed and tasks performed. An assessment of performance includes both attendance and punctuality as well.

## Using an Assessment Form

The assessment is made using the following scale:

O = outstanding (to an excellent degree)

G = good (to a degree above what is usually expected)

S = satisfactory (to a degree usually expected)

NI = needs improvement (below a degree that is acceptable)

U = unsatisfactory (far below acceptable performance)

In addition, the section for comments may be used to clarify the particular rating given for each criterion.

The assessment should be completed by the professional teacher with input from the teacher assistant. Whenever possible, agreement should be reached before a rating is assigned. The assessment should be signed and dated by both the professional teacher and the teacher assistant and then submitted to you. When differences about the ratings arise, you may want to participate in helping the teacher and the teacher assistant reach agreement.

# Supervising Student Teachers

A field experience component is required by virtually all teacher preparation programs. Students involved in these programs are known by a variety of titles, such as student teachers, associate teachers, or teacher interns.

## FACTORS THAT DETERMINE YOUR USE OF STUDENT TEACHERS

In general, college or university students in teacher preparation programs must successfully complete a field experience before they qualify for license, certification, or examination.

### Time Factor

The length of time for the students' direct involvement in the schools varies with the teacher-training institution and the type of certification or license sought. In general, students are involved directly in classrooms for one semester. During that time, the students may change their placement at least once to gain variety in the experience.

## Preparation

These students have completed course work in educational theory, methods, and subject content. The field experience provides two opportunities: (1) to observe and participate in an actual school setting, and (2) to apply theories and methods learned to a practical setting.

# THE ROLES OF THE STUDENT TEACHER, TEACHER, SUPERVISOR, AND COLLEGE SUPERVISOR

The student teacher, professional teacher, supervisor, and university or college supervisor all collaborate to make the field experience significant and mutually rewarding.

## The Student Teacher

The university or college program should define the objectives to be met by the student teacher during the school-based experience. Although these objectives may vary to some degree, they usually include the instructional, management, and professional aspects of teaching. (See Figure 25-1.)

**Instructional Aspects.** While participating in instructional activities, student teachers should demonstrate a knowledge of the subject or grade to which they are assigned. This includes an understanding of the scope and sequence of the specific content.

Involvement in instruction should include locating, organizing, preparing, and using a wide range of materials and equipment. This requirement gives experience in encouraging youngsters to be interested in and enthusiastic about learning.

The instructional techniques practiced should communicate with the class in an informative and manageable way. This requires that the wide range of individual differences found among any group of youngsters be diagnosed and then provided for with appropriate solution strategies.

Questioning strategies are an essential element of instruction. Student teachers should develop the ability to ask questions that stimulate critical thinking and analysis of material.

Assessment of students' progress is the natural outcome of instruction and is the means by which new activities are planned. An overview of the variety of assessment techniques available should be part of the instructional plan for every student teacher.

Figure 25-1

## THE ROLE OF THE STUDENT TEACHER

### Instructional Aspects

Understands:
    the scope of the subject or the grade to which assigned
    the sequence of the content

Instructional Materials Are:
    located
    organized

Uses a Variety of Instructional:
    materials and equipment
    approaches
    alternatives to provide for individual differences

Questioning Techniques Promote:
    clarification of concepts
    critical thinking
    analysis of materials

Assessment Techniques:
    are used to diagnose student progress
    are used to plan new activities

### Management Aspects

Planning:
    instructional time used effectively
    instructional time used efficiently

Classroom:
    demonstrates respect for the rights and dignity of all
    maintains good discipline
    attractive and comfortable

Records Are Kept:
    accurately
    appropriately
    in timely fashion

### Professional Aspects

Positive Interaction:
    with parents
    with the community

Attitude:
    ongoing self-development
    interest in keeping current with educational literature

**Management Aspects.** Student teachers should develop skills in planning to use time effectively and efficiently. Activities should be organized to maximize available instructional time.

The classroom should be structured around democratic principles that provide for the rights and dignity of all participants. Student teachers should learn how this is accomplished and maintained.

Well-functioning classrooms have standards for behavior and involvement that benefit all. The strategies required to involve all students in developing and practicing this code is an essential element in the education of teachers.

Student teachers should be involved in activities that will prepare them to design and implement comfortable, attractive, and healthful learning environments. Appealing classrooms encourage student activity.

Maintaining appropriate records and completing reports are important professional activities. Student teachers should have experience with preparing and understanding this aspect of teaching.

**Professional Aspects.** Interaction with parents and the community in general are a part of the professional role of the teacher. Student teachers should have the opportunity to observe and model this behavior.

Student teachers should be encouraged to develop a professional attitude about their work. This involves self-evaluation of their performance and a desire to improve.

Professional teachers and those preparing for a professional role must be interested in current and significant developments in the field of education. This includes the investigation of research results and field literature.

## The Professional Teacher

The involvement of a student teacher in the classroom of the professional teacher is both an asset and a responsibility. By observing and participating in classroom activities, student teachers perform valuable services for the teacher. But the professional teacher has the burden of providing meaningful opportunities through which the student teacher may learn. In addition, the teacher must offer guidance, suggestions, and directions that will benefit the student teacher.

**Instructional Aspects.** The student teaching experience begins most effectively by observing the behavior of the professional teacher. Using the teacher's directions, the student teacher should first begin to instruct individuals, then small groups, and finally the whole class in review and reinforcement activities. Experiences in teaching new content should be developed in the same sequence, beginning with individual students, such as those who were absent for the lesson. Then, small groups that may be advanced and able to move more quickly than their peers, should be instructed. After these experiences, the student teacher should be prepared to instruct the whole class in a new concept or skill.

The use of instructional materials should also be undertaken in developmental stages. The student teacher should first use those materials identified and prepared by the teacher. After experiencing the use of those instructional materials and their effect on the learning process, the student teacher should select, organize, and use instructional materials without assistance.

Instructional experiences may be broadened for student teachers by providing opportunities for them to take responsibility for a particular content area or topic under study. For example, the student teacher may take responsibility for teaching the skill of outlining to a seventh-grade English class, or for teaching the unit on the Civil War to a fifth-grade class.

As another alternative, the student teacher may wish to design a topic for study outside the regular curriculum. This topic or area may be one in which the student teacher has a particular skill or interest, such as figure drawing, writing poetry, or studying a specific event in the news.

These broadened instructional opportunities should involve the student teacher in planning, identifying, and selecting materials, organizing for instruction, and evaluating results.

**Management Aspects.**  By observing and conferring with the teacher, the student teacher sees specific examples of what and how the teacher plans for the instruction of students. Practical application in preparing plans may be experienced by the student teacher as preparations are made for areas of specific responsibility. The student teacher should ask for the advice and opinion of the professional teacher as the plans are developed.

As the student teacher assumes more responsibility in the classroom, opportunities will be present for experiences with discipline and humanistic approaches to the students. Continued activities will provide the student teacher with the refinement of skills in these areas.

The student teacher may be provided with opportunities to prepare an attractive and comfortable classroom as materials for instruction are created. Student products that result from the efforts may be placed on display around the room. The teacher may want to assign particular bulletin board space to the student teacher so that experience can be gained in organizing and mounting displays of students' work.

Student teachers should be provided with the opportunity to view, understand, and make entries on official records. The variety of records with which they should become acquainted include cumulative records, test cards, health data reports, attendance procedures, and report-to-parents forms. Other types of official and unofficial communications about students include anecdotal records, reports to the guidance counselor, and responses to parents' notes.

**Professional Aspects.**  Interaction with parents and the community is a sensitive area. Student teachers should have the opportunity to observe parent/teacher conferences and understand how they are conducted. However, if the parent wishes to speak directly with the teacher without the student teacher in attendance, this opportunity should be given and the sensitivity of the parent respected. Experience in conferring with parents can be simulated in role-playing situations with other student teachers.

Specific guidelines for conferring with parents should be discussed with the student teacher. Here is a set of guidelines:

1. Be friendly. Put the parent at ease.
2. Begin on a positive note. Say something nice about the child.
3. Listen to the parent. Pay attention and be sympathetic.
4. Sit at a student desk or a round table. Remove the authority symbol that the teacher's desk represents.
5. Do not ask prying questions of a personal nature.
6. Be prepared to document what you say about the youngster. Have records and samples of work available.
7. Prepare an outline of what you want to say in advance.
8. Speak simply and in plain language that is easily understood.
9. Focus on solutions. Criticism should be followed by specific suggestions for improvement. Form a cooperative plan.
10. Concentrate on the most important points of concern. Do not overwhelm the parent with multiple problems too numerous to be dealt with at the same time.
11. Do not argue or complain. Parents expect teachers to deal with the situation.
12. Leave lines of communication open. Indicate future contacts.

A professional attitude is best communicated and developed in student teachers by example. Hopefully, the attitudes of ongoing self-development and interest in professional topics and literature will be observed by student teachers as they listen to teachers interact in formal and informal ways. Situations that provide this opportunity include grade conferences, department conferences, faculty meetings, preparation periods, and the lunch period.

**Hints for Success.** Working toward the professional development of a student teacher is a big responsibility. The following hints are intended to help make the experience positive and rewarding.

When working with a student teacher, the professional teacher should —

1. Be specific about instructions and assignments
2. Follow through on suggestions, instructions, and promises
3. Constructively criticize in a humane manner
4. Set guidelines for participation
5. Establish time frames for specific activities
6. Confer frequently with the student teacher
7. Confer with the university supervisor about the student teacher
8. Be open and receptive to requests and suggestions
9. Be honest and professional in attitude and reactions

## The Supervisor

Your actions contribute greatly to the quality and success of the student teacher's involvement in the school. The performance of your role requires you to interact with all of the individuals who have a part in the total experience provided for the student teacher.

**Setting the Tone of the Experience.** You will probably be the first person to meet and greet the student teacher(s). Your greeting should be warm and cordial, making the individual or group feel welcome and wanted.

It may be wise to designate someone to act as the liaison between the student teacher, the professional teacher, the university or college supervisor, and the school. You may assign this duty to an assistant principal, guidance counselor, or teacher, as an administrative task. The person selected should be interested in this type of work and skillful at human relations. After greeting the student teachers, you will want to introduce the liaison and explain that person's role and responsibility.

Since the student teachers are new to the school organization and must quickly learn about it to function well, it is a good idea to give them a prepared handbook that explains the school. The handbook is best prepared by a committee that can also suggest what should be included. The specific content of the school handbook for student teachers will, of course, vary with the details of each individual school, but Figure 25-2 offers a suggested table of contents.

**Assigning the Student Teacher.** The assignment of the student teacher to a specific professional teacher is an important task. Several factors should be considered before the decision is made:

1. The type of assignment required by the university or college—Determine if the student teacher should be involved in primary grades, intermediate grades, the English or social studies department, and so forth.

2. The type of experience expected by the university or college—Determine if the student teacher should experience students of superior achievement, remedial needs, or a combination of both.

3. The personalities of the student teacher and the professional teacher—Identify and discuss with the university or college supervisor whether the student teacher is basically an introvert or extrovert. Seek a good match in personality from among the school staff.

4. The receptiveness of the professional teacher—Identify those professional teachers interested in working with student teachers. No staff member should be forced into a student teacher relationship.

5. A sensitivity to the needs of particular staff members, students, and programs—Give preference to identified problems. These may include classes with large registers, students with special needs grouped into a particular class, the personal or health needs of a staff member who may require assistance, or the personal or health needs of a staff member who cannot currently perform the required role.

**Figure 25-2**

---

### STUDENT TEACHER HANDBOOK

Table of Contents

Introduction and Welcome

The School

    Instructional Staff
    Service Staff
    Student Body
    Community
    Special Programs

Identification of Roles

    The Principal
    The Professional Teacher Assigned
    The University Supervisor
    The Student Teacher
    The Student Body
    The Parents
    The Staff

School Routines and Procedures

    Time Schedule
    Lunch Schedule
    Obtaining Materials
    Parking
    Special Considerations
    Special Opportunities

---

**Developing a Relationship With the University or College Supervisor.** An atmosphere of mutual benefit and involvement should be established between you and the student teacher's college supervisor. Both of you should talk openly and honestly about how each program, the student teacher, and the school can help one another. A climate of mutual commitment and concern should be established as a future means of solving problems that may present themselves.

**Opening Communication Lines.** Specific procedures for communication between the university or college supervisor and the involved professional teacher should be established. These procedures should be mutually convenient and valuable.

The line of communication between the college or university supervisor and the designated liaison should be clarified. Specific areas of responsibility and authority should be identified.

A direct line of communication between yourself and the university or college supervisor should also be stated and maintained.

## The College or University Supervisor

Hopefully, this individual is concerned about and sensitive to the particular needs and opportunities present in the school. This point of view will contribute to a maximally beneficial relationship.

The college supervisor should be cooperative and flexible in attempting to meet the needs of the student teachers within the possibilities provided by the school. Areas of disagreement should be discussed and a mutually agreed-upon solution reached.

The college or university supervisor has the responsibility of evaluating the work of the student teacher. However, the professional teacher working with the student teacher should be consulted throughout the experience. The professional teacher has specific details about the daily performance of the student teacher and his or her interaction and effectiveness with the youngsters. Suggestions for improvement should be shared with the supervisor so that consistent efforts are extended to the student teacher. In addition, the professional teacher should be consulted when a final evaluation is conducted so that an overview of the student teacher's work is provided.

# Supervising Volunteers

Unlike teacher assistants who are paid staff members, or student teachers whose work is required for certification or license, volunteers contribute to the school solely as a personal preference.

## CHARACTERISTICS OF VOLUNTEERS

School volunteers come from all ages, walks of life, and backgrounds. They represent housewives, high school and college students, parents, grandparents, and retirees from all fields. In general, the common link among this diverse group is that the people care about children and value education.

These exceptional people volunteer their service because they truly believe that their assistance can make a difference in the lives of the students with whom they work. Their reward is the self-satisfaction that comes from observing the youngsters with whom they work master skills, build self-confidence, develop positive attitudes toward school, and learn to trust and accept their world.

School volunteers provide an important link between the school and the community. They enter into a partnership dedicated to improving the educational opportunities of individual youngsters. Therefore, they may be directly responsible for assisting individual youngsters in becoming responsible adults.

## HOW VOLUNTEERS PARTICIPATE IN ACTIVITIES

School volunteers participate in a variety of ways with individual students and school-related services. To fully utilize your volunteers, consider these types of assignments:

### One-to-One Tutors

Volunteers interact with individual students in a wide range of needed areas, such as reading, writing, mathematics, and English second language.

### Classroom Assistance

Volunteers' services may be used to assist primary teachers in meeting the physical and material needs of young children; however, classroom involvement of school volunteers must be based on the teacher's acceptance and agreement. Often, the parent of a young child will volunteer to work in that child's classroom. When such a request is made, the teacher should be consulted as to the benefit and feasibility of such participation.

### School Programs

School volunteers may provide assistance with school services, including the library, the lunchroom, the bookroom, security, and the office.

### Special Programs

Volunteers may offer their specialized skills and abilities as mentors to the youngsters. In this way, students may learn about such topics as art forms, music, stamps, the stock market, and the like.

## PREPARING VOLUNTEERS FOR THE CLASSROOM

In large urban areas, school volunteers may be provided with training activities through organized volunteer programs. In areas where no such organization exists, schools may prepare volunteers by conducting a series of workshops that provide the rationale, guidelines, and specifics of their participation.

## THE SCHOOL'S ROLE WHEN USING VOLUNTEERS

To ensure that the school's relationship with the volunteer is mutually rewarding, several things must be kept in mind when working with volunteers.

### Accepting the Volunteer

The only payment school volunteers expect or require is a "thank you," respectful treatment, appreciation, and recognition. Very often, all that is needed is a friendly "hello" and a personal greeting when the volunteer arrives.

### Assigning the Volunteer

Care should be taken to meaningfully assign the school volunteer to an activity or role that he or she is capable and willing to perform. Time should be devoted to discussing possible involvements with the volunteer and identifying the one that will be most beneficial.

IMPORTANT: School volunteers are well intended and well meaning, but their services are dependent on their interest and ability to participate; therefore, their attendance may be inconsistent. Whenever possible, the volunteers' classroom activities should be *supplementary* rather than primary in the lives of the students with whom they interact.

### Designating a School Liaison

A school liaison should be designated and informed about the number and roles of the volunteers in the school. New volunteers can then be easily involved in areas that are not currently serviced.

The school liaison should also be able to monitor the quality and consistency of the volunteers' work. Suggestions, changes, and alternative involvements can be accomplished. When a central volunteer agency is involved, the school liaison can provide a communication link.

Any staff member with the interest and the time may be assigned as the school volunteer liaison. This includes the assistant principal, guidance counselor, special program teacher, or a classroom teacher.

# How to Supervise Nonteaching Personnel

# Supervising School Aides

Nonteaching personnel are an important consideration since in the performance of their roles, they provide services that directly or indirectly impact on the lives and, therefore, on the learning of students.

School aides are employed to provide the school with noninstructional services that support teacher efforts by eliminating their involvement in clerical and monitorial duties.

## THE SERVICES PERFORMED BY SCHOOL AIDES

School aides provide services that directly impact on the students' learning environment. A partial listing of their involvement follows.

### Health-Related Services

School aides may be responsible for monitoring immunization records. They may also bring the records of students with particular health-related disabilities to the school nurse.

## Attendance

Parent notification of absence may be performed by school aides. This may be accomplished by completing a post card or making a phone call. The school aide may be responsible for completing a truancy form in the case of a continued student absence.

## Lunch Money

School aides are usually involved with the collection, recordkeeping, and deposit of the school's lunch funds.

## Office Work

Important office services are often performed by school aides. They may answer telephones, file reports, and assist in securing information needed for ordering.

## Instructional Materials

School aides are often responsible for filling teachers' requests for books, supplies, materials, and media from bookrooms and supply closets. They may also maintain those books, supplies, materials, and media in good order with notations on a master inventory.

## Library Work

Maintaining the library in good working order by shelving, repairing, and displaying books may involve school aide assistance.

## Reproducing Materials

Operating rexograph, mimeograph, and copy machines that duplicate teacher-designed instructional materials is a major task assigned to school aides.

## Lunchroom Program

School aides are normally involved in assisting with the lunch program by seating youngsters, helping them to receive food and dispose of trash, and directing the movement of students into and out of the lunchroom.

## Bus Program

Assisting students to board, disembark, and use the bus in safety are important activities of school aides.

# THE SCHOOL AIDES' RELATIONSHIP TO INSTRUCTION

The impact of the services of school aides on the instructional life of students is obvious. First, they release the instructional staff from these tasks and therefore increase their time with the students.

Next, school aides perform services that relate to the health and safety of the students. These activities include the bus program, attendance, the lunch program, and health-related services.

Last, school aides directly affect the instructional life of students by responding to the teachers' requests for books, supplies, materials, and duplicated papers.

# MONITORING PERFORMANCE

The role of school aides in schools today has grown in importance. They should, therefore, be supervised to ensure quality work, time efficiency, punctuality, good attendance, and positive interpersonal relationships.

You may assume the responsibility for supervision of the school aides or you may delegate it to an assistant. Supervision of the performance of school aides may be accomplished by monitoring their movement, observing them in action, or investigating the time lapse between a request and its response.

Improvement in the performance of the services of school aides should, of course, relate to the identified problem. In general, however, their services may be improved by direct conferences, workshops or training programs, assigning a buddy to provide support, written communication, modification of their time schedules, or modification of their assigned tasks.

A sample school aide assignment plan is shown in Figure 27-1.

### Figure 27-1

**School Aide Assignment Plan**

| NAME | HOURS | BREAK | DUTIES |
|------|-------|-------|--------|
| Temi | 8:30-1:30 | 10:00-10:30 | —collect, count, deposit lunch funds<br>—maintain immunization records<br>—maintain health records<br>—bus duty A.M.<br>—lunch duty* |
| Gert | 9:00-2:00 | 9:45-10:15 | —assist in ordering<br>—distribute, repair equipment<br>—office assistance<br>—lunch duty* |
| Irene | 9:00-2:30 | 10:30-11:00 | —library shelving, repair<br>—maintain library records<br>—fill teacher requests for media<br>—maintain media inventory<br>—lunch duty* |
| Carole | 9:00-2:00 | 10:45-11:15 | —fill teacher requests for books and supplies<br>—maintain book inventory<br>—office assistance<br>—absentee notification<br>—lunch duty* |
| Gladys | 10:00-3:00 | 1:30-2:00 | —duplicate materials<br>—bus duty P.M.<br>—lunch duty* |

*lunch duty includes:
seating students
assisting in food distribution
assisting in disposing of trash
monitoring students' movement

# Supervising the Food Service Staff

The school food service staff impacts directly and significantly on students' learning in two ways. First, hungry youngsters are not involved in learning. Second, socially accepted habits of eating are learned in the lunchroom and reflect, in great measure, the manner in which the food is prepared and presented.

## HOW THE FOOD STAFF HELPS THE SCHOOL

The food personnel perform two services for the school: (1) selecting the menu, and (2) presenting the food.

### Menu Selection

The food selected for the lunch program should be nutritious and planned with a knowledge of the basic food requirements of youngsters. In addition, the dishes served should be appealing to the students. Whenever possible, foods should be selected because of their acceptance by the youngsters.

Provision should be made for students with individual dietary needs due to health restrictions or religious observance. Alternatives to the main course should be available on a daily basis.

## Food Presentation

The food should be prepared and presented to maximize visual appeal. It should be served with care and importance so that the youngsters develop positive attitudes about eating.

# IMPROVING THE SERVICES OF THE FOOD STAFF

The establishment of a nutrition committee is an effective tool in the continuing improvement of the food service program. The committee should be representative of the school population, including students selected by their peers, interested parents, the kitchen supervisor, a teacher representative, and a supervisor or a coordinator designated by the principal.

The committee should meet once a month to discuss problems and propose solutions that will improve the food service program. A sample nutrition committee agenda is given in Figure 28-1.

# MONITORING PERFORMANCE

The performance of the school food service staff should be monitored periodically. This activity may be conducted by the supervisor or the designated coordinator. Items to note include presentation of the food, serving procedures, alternatives to the main selection, and staff attitude toward the students.

Improvement in services performed may be accomplished by specific and detailed suggestions, modeling desired actions, requesting the involvement of the food services supervisor, changing time schedules, and altering task assignments.

**Figure 28-1**

NUTRITION COMMITTEE AGENDA
November 19xx


In attendance: Ms. King, coordinator
Mr. Muller, teacher
Ms. Standard, kitchen supervisor
Mrs. Gainly, parent
Bobbie Roberts, student
Juanita Rivera, student
Carl Washington, student


Agenda items: 1. variety of the menu
2. introduction of salad as an alternative
3. student manners and behavior
4. celebrating holidays in the lunchroom

# Supervising the School Plant Staff

The services provided by the school plant staff provide a clean, safe, warm, and comfortable environment. These factors directly impact on students and their desire to learn.

## THE ACTIVITIES OF THE SCHOOL PLANT STAFF

The plant staff is responsible for the complete maintenance of the school building and grounds. (Sample work schedules are given in Figures 29-1, 29-2, and 29-3.) The following are some of the plant staff's duties.

### Security

The plant staff is responsible for securing the building after school hours to prevent intruders from entering. They also open the buildings in the morning to provide for access by students and staff. This includes proper maintenance of the doors and security gates so that they open and close properly.

## Heating

The maintenance of an efficiently functioning boiler fired to assure building warmth and hot water in time for morning activities is an essential task.

## Cleanliness

The cleanliness of classrooms, halls, staircases, offices, toilets, and large assembly areas such as the auditorium, gymnasium, and lunchroom, are major activities for the school plant staff. These activities also involve the collection, packing, and disposal of garbage.

## Repairs and Supplies

The school plant staff is involved with the repair and maintenance of the school building on a continuing basis. This includes replacing light bulbs, repairing leaks, replacing broken windows, repairing and painting cracks, replacing broken floor tiles, maintaining the grounds surrounding the school, supplying toilet paper and towels, and so forth.

# MONITORING PERFORMANCE

The work of the school plant staff may be monitored by your observing the building on a continuing basis during informal inspection walks and by the staff's reporting observed needs to you in writing.

An open communication link should be maintained between you and the custodian in charge of the plant staff. Requests for repairs and improvement of services should be made by you in writing to the custodian. If you keep a dated copy of the request, you will be able to check the completion of the task after a reasonable period of time has passed. See Figure 29-4 for a sample request form.

When improvement of services is desired, you may discuss the concerns with the custodian in a formal meeting, write the concerns in a formal letter to the custodian, request the involvement of the custodian's supervisor, suggest modification in the time schedule of duties, or recommend changes in the assignment of individual staff members.

Figure 29-1

## School Plant Staff Work Schedule

**Name:** John MacMurray
**Title:** Fireman/Handyman
**Hours of Work:** 7:00 A.M. to 4:00 P.M.

| Time | Job Assignment |
|------|----------------|
| 7:00-8:30 | Clean oil strainers<br>Clean rotary cup<br>Start Boiler(s)<br>Start Gymnasium, Cafeteria, Auditorium Exhausters<br>Turn on all lights throughout the building including all toilets<br>Turn on all toilet exhausters<br>Start Gymnasium, Cafeteria, Auditorium Blowers<br>Remove all locking devices from exit doors<br>Physically check each basement room for signs of entry<br>Report same to Custodian<br>Note any burned out fixtures in basement section<br>Open all cross corridor doors and security gates |
| 8:30-9:00 | Clean students' cafeteria after breakfast program<br>Clean assigned stairs |
| 9:00-9:15 | Coffee Break |
| 9:15-10:00 | Preventative Maintenance in Boiler Room and Fan Rooms<br>Check belts for signs of wear<br>Lubricate equipment when and where necessary |
| 10:00-11:00 | Work Assigned by Custodian |
| 11:00-12 Noon | Lunchtime |
| 12 Noon-1:00 | Replace burned out fixtures in Basement Section |
| 1:00-2:30 | Work Assigned by Custodian |
| 2:30-2:45 | Coffee Break |
| 2:45-4:00 | Clean Basement Section<br>Secure all outside exit doors |

## Figure 29-2

### School Plant Staff Work Schedule

**Name:**  Peter Negron
**Title:**  Cleaner
**Hours of Work:**  8:00 A.M. to 5:00 P.M.

| Time | Job Assignment |
|------|----------------|
| 8:00-9:00 | Put up flag<br>Sweep stairs<br>Clean auditorium<br>Begin outside grounds clean up |
| 9:00-9:15 | Coffee Break |
| 9:15-11:00 | Continue outside grounds clean up<br>Work assigned by the Custodian |
| 11:00-12 Noon | Replace burned out fixtures on first floor<br>Work assigned by Custodian |
| 12 Noon-1:00 | Lunchtime |
| 1:00-2:00 | Clean cafeteria |
| 2:00-2:30 | Work assigned by Custodian |
| 2:30-2:45 | Coffee Break |
| 2:45-5:00 | Clean first floor<br>Secure building<br>Activate intrusion alarm |

### Figure 29-3

**School Plant Staff Work Schedule**

**Name:** James Dancer
**Title:** Cleaner
**Hours of Work:** 1:00 P.M. to 5:00 P.M.

| Time | Job Assignment |
|------|----------------|
| 1:00-1:30 | Clean stairs<br>Replace burned out fixtures on second floor<br>Work assigned by Custodian |
| 1:30-2:30 | Clean cafeteria<br>Sweep and mop all spills<br>Remove all garbage |
| 2:30-2:45 | Coffee Break |
| 2:45-4:00 | Clean second floor section |
| 4:00-5:00 | Bag garbage for all sections |

### Figure 29-4

**MEMO**

To: _____, custodian

From: _____, (title)

Re: Request for services

Date: _____

Please respond. Request completed on _____

# Supervising the Secretarial Staff

School secretaries perform a multitude of support services for the school that interact directly and indirectly with the lives of students and, therefore, with their instructional needs.

## WHY A GOOD SECRETARIAL STAFF IS IMPORTANT

The activities of the school secretaries touch every member of the school population. The range of their activities includes preparation and distribution of payroll as well as public relations.

### Office Reception

Everyone who enters the building should be directed to the office, where the visitors are greeted by the school secretaries. Each person who enters the office should be given assistance within a few moments after arrival. Office personnel should be aware of people entering during the day and greet these people with an appropriate statement such as "Good morning (afternoon). May I help you?" Every effort should be made to be polite and courteous with all requests.

As a general rule, people other than school staff should not be permitted to go to the classrooms without an arranged appointment with the teacher. Parents' requests for homework or student pickup can be met by sending a message to the appropriate classroom while the parent waits in the office. Allowing parents to walk unannounced into classrooms while teachers are involved with students can cause disruption of classes and possible problems.

## Telephone Reception

For many people, a telephone response is the first contact with the school, which is why the telephone response should be organized and structured. Callers should immediately know that they have reached the correct number and that the person answering the telephone wants to be of assistance.

After greeting the caller, the secretary must then make a decision about the response. Requests to speak with teachers who are involved with students must be postponed with a suggestion about when and how the contact may be made. Requests to speak with you will depend upon your availability and efficiency in taking the call. Certainly, calls that are received while you are in conference, on the telephone, or with individuals should be received by the secretary with a message taken. Calls that can be handled by the secretaries or other personnel should be taken care of without your involvement.

## Teacher Substitutes

Unless this is centrally controlled, school secretaries may be responsible for receiving the phone calls of teachers who will be absent, and then securing a day-to-day substitute. If this function is controlled centrally, the secretaries are responsible for maintaining the attendance records for the teachers.

When a substitute is located to fulfill the responsibilities of the absent teacher, the secretary is responsible for transferring information to the substitute about the school and the specific tasks expected of him or her. In addition, any information that the substitute is required to supply at the end of the day will be given to a secretary for later transmission to the teacher who has returned from the absence.

## Payroll

A school secretary prepares the payroll reports for all staff members and is, therefore, responsible for their completion and accuracy. When payroll is received, it is usually the secretary who checks the printout and distributes the checks.

## School Mail

The secretary is directly responsible for the large volume of mail sent by and received at the school. It is the secretary who receives, sorts, and distributes the mail. In addition, school secretaries prepare outgoing school correspondence with appropriate return address and postage.

## Reports

The secretaries are responsible for preparing reports that are due on a periodic basis. These reports should be signed by you so you can check their accuracy and the fact that they have been prepared.

Other reports that require your preparation are also completed by the school secretaries. The secretaries must be accurate and neat in their completion of the data you have given them.

## Correspondence

Your correspondence with the outside world is controlled by the school secretaries who type your messages. In general, you may be judged by the neatness, punctuality, and accuracy of that work.

## Admission and Discharge of Students

The school secretaries are responsible for the accurate and efficient handling of the procedures involved in admitting students to and discharging students from the school. Complaints about problems in the performance of these tasks will be reported to you.

# THE SECRETARIES'
# RELATIONSHIP TO INSTRUCTION

Since the role of the school secretaries is comprehensive, it affects every member of the school population—including students. When a teacher is disturbed by a parent, for example, the conduct of instruction in the class is interrupted. Teachers who have payroll concerns are not necessarily totally involved in the day-to-day performance of their tasks.

The public relations aspect of the secretarial role is paramount in the reputation of the school. Since the secretaries meet and greet the community in person and on the telephone, their attitude and interest set the image of the school in the mind of the public.

The punctuality and accuracy of the reports and paperwork that are completed and prepared by the school secretaries reflect the image of the school as an efficient and effective organization. In reality, since you are responsible for all activities that are performed, *your* reputation as an administrator and supervisor may be transmitted through the performance of the secretaries.

## MONITORING PERFORMANCE

The work of the school secretaries is your responsibility. Be aware of reports and correspondence that are due, and remind the secretaries of these due dates and notes.

In addition, you should review reports that are prepared before they are signed so that you are sure nothing inaccurate or inappropriate is sent.

The services of the school secretaries may be improved by informal discussions, formal letters of suggestions, or redistribution of tasks, roles, and responsibilities.

# Index